From Prof D[illegible]

THE REVIVALIST:

A NEW

SELECTION OF HYMNS AND SPIRITUAL SONGS,

DESIGNED FOR THE USE OF

Conference Meetings, Private Circles,

AND

THE CLASS ROOM.

By WASHINGTON GLASS.

"I will sing with the Spirit and with the understanding."

FIRST EDITION.

COLUMBUS:
PRINTED BY SCOTT & BASCOM.
1853.

SCOTT & BASCOM,
Stereotypers and Binders,
COLUMBUS.

PREFACE.

The design of this small work is, in the first place, to add to the life and spirituality of the Class Room and the Prayer Meeting, and also for Conference, and for Revivals of Religion. This, at the same time, being a pocket companion to all Christians, in public or in the closet. The author has taken all pains possible to bring before the public a work that will please his patrons; and also hoping that when the hymns and songs are repeated, the happy Christian may rejoice in view of that rest which remains for the people of God.

The question has been asked, Can we not have a small hymn book to be used in time of Revivals of Religion? This work contains many pieces that were never before the public previous to this. The author has selected from about thirty different works. This he did for the advancement and progress of the cause of God. To get up a work of this character, is to give every Christian an opportunity of singing the songs that this work contains. May every professor seek for a copy of this work, and examine it with a prayerful heart. May the great Spirit cause a reformation in the heart of the poor sinner when these hymns are sung.

WASHINGTON GLASS.

INDEX OF FIRST LINES.

A charge to keep I have.............................. 28
A few more days on earth to spend.................... 56
After we list the seraphs' lays........................112
Alas! and did my Saviour bleed...................... 21
All hail the power of Jesus' name....................165
Amazing grace! how sweet the sound................. 62
Am I a soldier of the cross.......................... 90
And must this body die.............................126
A poor wayfaring man of grief....................... 31
Approach, my soul, the mercy seat................... 16
Arise and shine, O Zion fair..........................106
As on the cross the Saviour hung....................184
A story most lovely I'll tell.............. 189
At anchor laid, remote from home.................... 88
Awake, my soul, in joyful lays....................... 39

Behold the Saviour of mankind...................... 29
Blow ye the trumpet, blow.......................... 10
Brethren, while we sojourn here...................... 43
Broad is the road that leads to death................ 63

Children of the heavenly King...................... 22
Come sound his praise abroad........................ 2
Come let us join, our Lord to praise.................. 4
Come, Holy Spirit, heavenly dove.................... 7
Come, ye sinners, poor and needy.................... 9
Come let us join our cheerful songs.................. 19
Come, thou everlasting Spirit........................ 30
Come, thou fount of every blessing.................. 42
Come, we that love the Lord.........................166
Come, humble sinner, in whose breast................ 54
Come on, my partners in distress..................... 85
Come, ye that fear the Lord, unto me.................135
Come, sisters and brothers, who love one another......178
Come, brothers and sisters, and hear me relate........192
Come listen to my story.............................212

Depth of mercy, can there be........................ 4
Did Christ o'er sinners weep........................ 5

Farewell, dear friends, I must be gone................ 35
Farewell, loving Christian, the time is at hand........ 59
Farewell, loved ones, death hath torn you............153
Farewell, vain world, I bid adieu.................... 64
Fast by the river's side, that flowed.................113
Father, I stretch my hands to thee.................. 36
From all that dwell below the skies.................. 3
From every stormy wind that blows.................. 92
From gloomy dejection my thoughts mount the sky... 89
From Greenland's icy mountains..................... 51
From all that dwell below the skies.................. 67

Hail, thou blest morn when the great Mediator........ 71
Hail, ye sighing sons of sorrow......................180
Hark, brethren! do n't you hear the sound 168
Hark! from the tombs, a doleful sound............... 16
Hark! do n't you hear the turtle dove................210
Hark, my soul! it is the Lord.........................182
Hark! ten thousand harps and voices 164
Hasten, Lord, the glorious time 46
He dies: the friend of sinners dies...................115
Holy Bible, book divine 8
How firm a foundation, ye saints of the Lord.......... 99
How happy are they 96
How lost was my condition 67
How lovely the place where the Saviour appears.......140
How happy is the man who has chosen wisdom's ways. 23
How tedious and tasteless the hours.................. 75
How happy every child of grace......................125
How sweet the name of Jesus sounds 147

I came to the spot where the white pilgrim lay 195
I have sought round this verdant earth...............101
I know that my Redeemer lives 6
I 'm glad that I am born to die 211
In all my Lord's appointed ways 93
In de dark woods, no Indian nigh....... 114
I would not live alway: I ask not to stay 79

Jerusalem, my happy home 122
Jesus, I my cross have taken 1
Jesus, my advocate on high.......................... 88

Jesus, my all, to heaven is gone....................158
Joyfully, joyfully, onward I move....................152
Joy to the world! the Lord is come.................. 26

Lord, at thy temple we appear....................183
Lord, dismiss us with thy blessing.................... 61

Majestic sweetness sits enthroned....................206
Mary to the Saviour's tomb....................157
Mid scenes of confusion and creature complaints...... 48
My Bible leads to glory.................... 86
My days, my weeks, my months, my years............ 70
My friends and my neighbors, who live in this place...185
My gracious Redeemer I love....................160
My soul, come meditate the day.................... 39
My soul forsakes her vain delights....................114

Now the Saviour standeth pleading.................. 34

O come, come away, from labor now reposing.........190
O'er the gloomy hills of darkness.................... 77
O for a closer walk with God.................... 13
O for a thousand tongues to sing.................... 17
O for a breeze of heavenly love....................108
Of Jesus Christ I 'm not ashamed.................... 78
O how charming....................109
O Jesus, my Saviour,.................... 84
O Jesus, my Saviour, I know thou art mine........... 95
One day, as I was walking, &c....................120
On Jordan's stormy banks I stand.................... 81
O that I had some humble place....................175
O that I knew the secret place.................... 12
O that my load of sin were gone.................... 15
O there will be mourning.................... 52
O thou in whose presence my soul takes delight.......104
Our bondage here shall end....................214
Our Lord is risen from the dead.................... 27
Our souls, by love together knit.................... 75
O when shall I see Jesus....................162
O ye young, ye gay, ye proud....................151

Pale, motionless and silent, lay....................187
Plung'd in a gulf of dark despair.................... 20

Religion is the chief concern.................... 27
Religion, what a glorious treasure....................144
Remember, sinful youth, you must die................218

Salvation! O the joyful sound........................ 25
Show pity, Lord! O Lord, forgive...................... 13
Since man, by sin, has lost his God...................140
Sing to the Lord, ye distant lands....................194
Sin hath a thousand treacherous arts.................106
Sinners! perhaps this news to you...................204
Sweet rivers of redeeming love.......................223

The chariot, the chariot, its wheels roll in fire......... 47
Thee we adore, eternal name.......................... 73
The day is past and gone............................. 50
The reason we love friendship........................154
There is a fountain filled with blood..................118
There is a happy land................................ 55
There is a land of pure delight.......................124
There is a path that leads to God..................... 37
The war in which the soldier fights...................206
The work of the Lord doth revive....................150
The voice of free grace..............................216
Thou art gone, little one, to a beautiful home.........221
Thus saith the Lord of glory..........................203
Time speeds away, away, away 171
'Tis low down in that beautiful valley 167
'Tis religion that can give 27
Together let us sweetly live.......................... 31
To leave my dear friends, and with neighbors to part .. 44
To thee, O my Saviour! to thee will I cling............138

We 're traveling home to heaven above................208
Well met, dear friends, in Jesus' name................ 63
What ship is this, that shall take us all home.........108
What 's this that steals away my breath.............. 65
What a mercy, a mercy is this........................145
When for eternal worlds we steer.....................132
When I call to my remembrance.......................172
When I can read my title clear....................... 18
When I first started away from you..................143
When I set out for glory.............................176
When I survey the wondrous cross....................220
When marshaled on the nightly plain................ 41
When the spark of life is waning..................... 76
When the waves of life o'ertake me.................. 53
When those we love are snatched away...............159
When torn is the bosom by sorrow or care............127

While nature was sinking in stillness to rest..........148
While wandering to and fro 133
Worthy, worthy is the Lamb.........................141
Why do we mourn departing friends.................. 74
Why should we start and fear to die.................. 38

Young ladies all, attention give 198
Young men and maids, where'er you be 136
Young people all, attention give.......................115
Young people who delight in sin......................156
You may sing of the beauty of mountains and glen....102

THE

REVIVALIST.

1.

8s & 7s.

1 JESUS, I my cross have taken,
All to leave and follow thee;
Naked, poor, despised, forsaken,
Thou from hence my all shalt be.
Perish every fond ambition,
All I 've sought, or hoped, or known,
Yet how rich is my condition,
God and heaven are all my own.

2 Let the world despise and leave me,
They have left my Saviour too;
Human hopes and looks deceive me,
Thou art not like them, untrue;
And while thou shalt smile upon me,
God of wisdom, love and might,
Friends may hate and foes may scorn me—
Show thy face and all is right.

3 Go, then, earthly fame and treasure,
Come disaster, scorn and pain;

In thy service pain is pleasure.
With thy favor loss is gain.
I have call'd thee, Abba, Father,
I have set my heart on thee,
Storms may howl and clouds may gather,
All must work for good to me.

4 Soul, then know thy full salvation,
Rise o'er sin, and fear, and care,
Joy to find in every station
Something still to do or bear.
Think what Spirit dwells within thee,
Think what heavenly bliss is thine,
Think that Jesus died to save thee—
Child of heaven, canst thou repine?

5 Haste thee on from grace to glory,
Armed by faith and wing'd by prayer;
Heaven's eternal day 's before thee;
God's own hand shall lead thee there.
Soon shall close thine earthly mission,
Soon shall pass thy pilgrim days;
Hope shall change to glad fruition,
Faith to sight, and prayer to praise.

2.

S. M.

1 COME sound his praise abroad,
And hymns of glory sing;

Jehovah is the Sovereign God,
The universal King.

2 He formed the deeps unknown,
He gave the seas their bound;
The watery worlds are all his own,
And all the solid ground.

3 Come worship at his throne,
Come bow before the Lord;
We are his works and not our own;
He formed us by his word.

4 To-day attend his voice,
Nor dare provoke his rod;
Come, like the people of his choice,
And own your gracious God.

3.

L. M.

1 FROM all that dwell below the skies
Let the Creator's praise arise,
Let the Redeemer's name be sung,
Through every land, by every tongue.

2 Eternal are thy mercies, Lord,
Eternal truth attends thy word,
Thy praise shall sound from shore to shore,
Till suns shall rise and set no more.

4.

C. M.

1 COME let us join, our Lord to praise,
Whose mercy knows no end,
To him our cheerful voices raise—
Our Father and our friend.

2 In tender infancy his care
Preserved our lives from harm,
And now he keeps us from the snare
Of sin's deceitful charm.

3 He gives us friends who seek our good,
And strive to make us wise ;
His bounteous hand provides our food,
And all our want supplies.

4 With grateful praise we will proclaim
The mercies of our God,
And sing the glory of his name,
Who bought us with his blood.

5.

4 lines 7s.

1 DEPTH of mercy, can there be
Mercy still reserved for me?
Can my God his wrath forbear,
Me, the chief of sinners, spare?

2 I have long withstood his grace,
Long provoked him to his face,
Would not hearken to his calls—
Griev'd him by a thousand falls.

3 Kindled his relentings are,
Me he now delights to spare,
Cries, "how shall I give thee up?"
Lets the lifted thunder drop.

4 There for me the Saviour stands—
Shows his wounds and spreads his hands;
God is love, I know, I feel,
Jesus weeps and loves me still.

5 Jesus, answer from above,
Is not all thy nature love?
Wilt thou not the wrong forget?
Suffer me to kiss thy feet.

6 Now incline me to repent,
Let me now my fall lament;
Now my foul revolt deplore,
Weep, believe, and sin no more.

6.

S. M.

1 DID Christ o'er sinners weep,
And shall our cheeks be dry?

Let floods of penitêntial grief
  Burst forth from every eye.

2 The Son of God in tears,
  Angels with wonder see ;
Be thou astonished, O, my soul,
  He shed those tears for me !

3 He wept that we might weep,
  Each sin demands a tear ;
In heaven alone no sin is found,
  And there 's no weeping there.

7.

L. M.

1 I KNOW that my Redeemer lives—
What comfort this sweet sentence gives;
He lives, he lives, who once was dead—
He lives, my ever-living head.

2 He lives to bless me with his love—
He lives to plead for me above;
He lives my hungry soul to feed,
He lives to help in time of need.

3 He lives to grant me rich supply,
He lives to guide me with his eye;
He lives to comfort me when faint,
He lives to hear my soul's complaint.

4 He lives to silence all my fears,
He lives to wipe away my tears;
He lives to calm my troubled heart,
He lives all blessings to impart.

5 He lives—all glory to his name;
He lives, my Jesus, still the same;
O, the sweet joy this sentence gives—
I know that my Redeemer lives.

8.

C. M.

1 COME, Holy Spirit, heavenly Dove,
With all thy quickening powers—
Kindle a flame of sacred love
In these cold hearts of ours

2 Look how we grovel here below—
Fond of these trifling toys;
Our souls can neither fly nor go,
To reach eternal joys.

3 In vain we tune our formal songs—
In vain we strive to rise;
Hosannas languish on our tongues,
And our devotion dies.

4 Dear Lord! and shall we ever live
At this poor dying rate;

Our love so faint, so cold to thee,
And thine to us so great?

5 Come, Holy Spirit, Heavenly Dove,
With all thy quickening powers;
Come, shed abroad a Saviour's love,
And that shall kindle ours.

9.

7s.

1 HOLY Bible, book divine,
Precious treasure, thou art mine!
Mine to tell me whence I came,
Mine to teach we what I am.

2 Mine to chide me when I rove,
Mine to show a Saviour's love;
Mine art thou to guide my feet,
Mine to judge, condemn, acquit.

3 Mine to comfort in distress,
If the Holy Spirit bless;
Mine to show by living faith,
Man can triumph over death.

4 Mine to tell of joys to come,
And the rebel sinner's doom;
O, thou precious book divine!
Precious treasure, thou art mine.

10.

P. M.

1 COME, ye sinners, poor and needy—
Weak and wounded, sick and sore—
Jesus ready stands to save you,
Full of pity, love and power:
He is able,
He is willing—doubt no more.

2 Now, ye needy, come and welcome—
God's free bounty glorify;
True belief and true repentance,
Every grace that brings you nigh:
Without money,
Come to Jesus Christ and buy.

3 Let not conscience make you linger,
Nor of fitness fondly dream;
All the fitness he requireth,
Is, to feel your need of him:
This he gives you—
'Tis the Spirit's glimmering beam.

4 Come, ye weary, heavy laden,
Bruis'd and mangled by the fall—
If you tarry till you're better,
You will never come at all:
Not the righteous—
Sinners Jesus came to call.

5 Agonizing in the garden,
  Lo, your Maker prostrate lies;
On the bloody tree behold him,
  Hear him cry before he dies:
    It is finish'd—
  Sinners will not this suffice?

6 Lo! the incarnate God ascending,
  Pleads the merit of his blood;
Venture on him—venture freely,
  Let no other trust intrude:
    None but Jesus
  Can do helpless sinners good.

7 Saints and angels join'd in concert,
  Sing the praises of the Lamb—
While the blissful seats of heaven
  Sweetly echo with his name;
    Hallelujah—
  Sinners here may do the same.

11.

4 6s & 2 8s.

1 BLOW ye the trumpet, blow,
  The gladly solemn sound—
Let all the nations know,
  To earth's remotest bounds,
The year of jubilee is come,
Return, ye ransom'd sinners, home.

2 Jesus, our great High Priest,
  Hath full atonement made;
Ye weary spirits rest,
  Ye mournful souls be glad—
The year of jubilee is come,
Return, ye ransomed sinners, home.

3 Extol the Lamb of God,
  The all-atoning Lamb—
Redemption in his blood,
  Throughout the world proclaim—
The year of jubilee is come,
Return, ye ransom'd sinners, home.

4 Ye slaves of sin and hell,
  Your liberty receive,
And safe in Jesus dwell,
  And blest in Jesus live;
The year of jubilee is come,
Return, ye ransom'd sinners, home.

5 Ye who have sold for nought
  Your heritage above,
Shall have it back, unbought—
  The gift of Jesus' love;
The year of jubilee is come,
Return, ye ransom'd sinners. home.

6 The gospel trumpet hear,
The news of heavenly grace,
And, sav'd from earth, appear
Before your Saviour's face.
The year of jubilee is come,
Return, ye ransom'd sinners, home.

12.

C. M.

Seeking after God.

1 O, THAT I knew the secret place,
Where I might find my God;
I'd spread my wants before his face,
And pour my woes abroad.

2 I'd tell him how my sins arise,
What sorrows I sustain—
How grace decays, and comfort dies,
And leaves my heart in pain.

3 He knows what arguments I'd take,
To wrestle with my God;
I'd plead for his own mercy's sake,
And for my Saviour's blood.

4 My God will pity my complaints,
And heal my broken bones;
He knows the meaning of his saints—
The language of their groans.

5 Arise, my soul, from deep distress,
And banish every fear;
He calls thee to his throne of grace,
To spread thy sorrows there.

13.

L. M.

1 SHOW pity, Lord; O Lord, forgive—
Let a repenting rebel live;
Are not thy mercies large and free?
May not a sinner trust in thee?

2 O wash my soul from every sin,
And make my guilty conscience clean;
Here on my heart the burden lies—
And past offences pain my eyes.

3 My lips, with shame, my sins confess,
Against thy law—against thy grace;
Lord, should thy judgment grow severe,
I am condemned, but thou art clear.

4 Yet, save a trembling sinner, Lord, [word,
Whose hope, still hovering round thy
Would light on some sweet promise there,
Some sure support against despair.

14.

C. M.

1 O, FOR a closer walk with God,
A calm and heavenly frame—

A light to shine upon the road
That leads me to the Lamb.

2 Where is the blessedness I knew
When first I saw the Lord?
Where is the soul-refreshing view
Of Jesus and his word?

3 What peaceful hours I once enjoyed—
How sweet their memory still!
But they have left an aching void,
The world can never fill.

4 Return! O holy Dove, return!
Sweet messenger of rest;
I hate the sins that made thee mourn,
And drove thee from my breast.

5 The dearest idol I have known,
Whate'er that idol be,
Help me to tear it from thy throne,
And worship only thee.

6 So shall my walk be close with God,
Calm and serene my frame;
So purer light shall mark the road
That leads me to the Lamb.

15.

L. M.

1 O, THAT my load of sin were gone!
  O, that I could at last submit,
At Jesus' feet to lay it down—
  To lay my soul at Jesus' feet.

2 Rest for my soul, I long to find,
  Saviour of all, if mine thou art,
Give me thy meek and lowly mind,
  And stamp thine image on my heart.

3 Break off the yoke of inbred sin,
  And fully set my spirit free;
I cannot rest till pure within—
  Till I am wholly lost in thee.

4 Fain would I learn of thee, my God,
  Thy light and easy burden prove;
The cross all stain'd with hallow'd blood,
  The labor of thy dying love.

5 I would, but thou must give the power,
  My heart from every sin release;
Bring near, bring near the joyful hour,
  And fill me with thy perfect peace.

6 Come, Lord, the drooping sinner cheer,
  Nor let thy chariot wheels delay;

Appear in my poor heart, appear,
My God, my Saviour, come away.

16.

C. M.

1 HARK! from the tombs, a doleful sound;
Mine ears attend the cry;
Ye living men, come view the ground
Where you must shortly lie.

2 Princes, this clay must be your bed,
In spite of all your towers;
The tall, the wise, the reverend head
Shall lie as low as ours.

3 Great God, is this our certain doom?
And are we still secure?
Still walking downward to the tomb,
And yet prepared no more?

4 Grant us the power of quickening grace,
To fit our souls to fly;
Then when we drop this dying flesh
We'll rise above the sky.

17.

C. M.

The Mercy-Seat.

1 APPROACH, my soul, the mercy-seat,
Where Jesus answers prayer;

There humbly fall before his feet,
For none can perish there.

2 Thy promise is my only plea,
With this I venture nigh;
Thou callest burden'd souls to thee,
And such, O Lord, am I.

3 Bow'd down beneath a load of sin,
By Satan sorely press'd,
By wars without, and fears within,
I come to thee for rest.

4 Be thou my shield and hiding place;
That, shelter'd near thy side,
I may my fierce accuser face,
And tell him, "Thou hast died!"

5 Oh, wondrous love, to bleed and die,
To bear the cross and shame,
That guilty sinners, such as I,
Might plead thy gracious name.

18.

C. M.

1 O, for a thousand tongues to sing
My great Redeemer's praise,
The glories of my God and King—
The triumphs of his grace.

2 My gracious Master, and my God,
Assist me to proclaim,
To spread through all the earth abroad,
The honors of thy name.

3 Jesus! the name that charms our fears,
That bids our sorrows cease,
'Tis music in the sinner's ears—
'Tis life, and health, and peace.

4 He breaks the power of cancel'd sin,
He sets the prisoner free;
His blood can make the foulest clean,
His blood availed for me.

5 He speaks! and, listening to his voice,
New life the dead receive;
The mournful, broken hearts rejoice,
The humble poor believe.

6 Hear him, ye deaf; his praise, ye dumb,
Your loosened tongues employ;
Ye blind, behold your Saviour come,
And leap, ye lame, for joy.

19. C. M.

1 WHEN I can read my title clear,
To mansions in the skies,

I'll bid farewell to every fear,
And wipe my weeping eyes.

2 Should earth against my soul engage,
And fiery darts be hurl'd,
Then I can smile at Satan's rage,
And face a frowning world.

3 Let cares like a wild deluge come,
Let storms of sorrow fall;
So I but safely reach my home,
My God, my heaven, my all:

3 There I shall bathe my weary soul
In seas of heavenly rest,
And not a wave of trouble roll
Across my peaceful breast.

20.

C. M.

1 COME let us join our cheerful songs
With angels round the throne;
Ten thousand thousand are their tongues,
But all their joys are one.

2 Worthy the Lamb that died, they cry,
To be exalted thus—
Worthy the Lamb, our lips reply,
For he was slain for us.

3 Jesus is worthy to receive
Honor and power divine;
And blessings more than we can give,
Be, Lord, forever thine.

4 Let all that dwell above the sky,
And air, and earth, and seas,
Conspire to lift thy glories high,
And speak thine endless praise.

21. C. M.

1 PLUNG'D in a gulf of dark despair,
We wretched sinners lay,
Without one cheering beam of hope,
Or spark of glimmering day.

2 With pitying eyes the Prince of grace
Beheld our helpless grief;
He saw, and (O, amazing love,)
He ran to our relief.

3 Down from the shining seats above,
With joyful haste he fled,
Enter'd the grave in mortal flesh,
And dwelt among the dead.

4 O, for this love, let rocks and hills
Their lasting silence break,

And all harmonious human tongues
The Saviour's praises speak.

5 Angels assist our mighty joys—
Strike all your harps of gold;
But when you raise your highest notes,
His love can ne'er be told.

22.

C. M.

1 ALAS! and did my Saviour bleed?
And did my Sovereign die?
Would he devote that sacred head
For such a worm as I?

2 Was it for crimes that I have done,
He groaned upon the tree?
Amazing pity, grace unknown,
And love beyond degree!

3 Well might the sun in darkness hide,
And shut his glories in,
When Christ, the mighty Maker, died
For man, the creature's sin.

4 Thus might I hide my blushing face,
While his dear cross appears—
Dissolve my heart in thankfulness,
And melt mine eyes to tears.

5 But drops of grief can ne'er repay
The debt of love I owe;
Here, Lord, I give myself away,
'Tis all that I can do.

23.

4 lines 7s.

1 CHILDREN of the heavenly King,
As we journey, let us sing —
Sing our Saviour's worthy praise,
Glorious in his works and ways.

2 We are traveling home to God,
In the way the fathers trod;
They are happy now, and we
Soon their happiness shall see.

3 O, ye banished seed, be glad,
Christ, our advocate is made;
Us to save, our flesh assumes,
Brother to our souls becomes.

4 Fear not, brethren, joyful stand
On the borders of our land;
Jesus Christ, our Father's Son,
Bids us undismayed go on.

5 Lord, obediently we 'll go,
Gladly leaving all below;

Only thou our leader be,
And we still will follow thee.

24.

6s & 8s.

1 HOW happy is the man who has chosen wisdom's ways,
And has measured out his span to his God in prayer and praise;
His God and his Bible are all that he desires,
And to holiness of heart he continually aspires;
In poverty he 's happy, for he knows he has a friend
Who has promised to be with him till the world shall have an end.

2 He rises in the morning—with the lark he tunes his lays,
And offers up his tribute to his God in prayer and praise;
And then to his labor he cheerfully repairs,
In confidence believing that God will hear his prayers.
Whatever he engages in at home or abroad,
His object is to honor and to glorify his God.

3 He hails with joy the morning that rolls the Sabbath round,

And in the courts of worship he is ever to be found;
His seat at the church he is always sure to fill,
Low at the feet of Jesus, there to do his Master's will,
He claims his Father's promises, he freely did bestow,
His Son, the promotion of his righteousness below.

4 'Tis thus you have his history through life from day to day;
Religion is no mystery with him, 'tis to obey;
And then on his pillow he lays him down to die,
In confidence rejoicing, for he knows his God is nigh;
And when his lamp is faltering, his soul, on wings of love,
Flies to realms of glory, to dwell with Christ above.

5 His body then is laid in the cold and silent tomb,
There to rest, undisturbed, till resurrection morn;

And when the archangel shall sound the
dread alarm,
In triumph he arises to his blest Redeemer's arms;
In union with his brethren, he there resumes
his lays,
And offers up his tribute to his God in
prayer and praise.

25.

C. M.

1 SALVATION! O the joyful sound,
'Tis pleasure to our ears;
A sovereign balm for every wound,
A cordial for our fears.

2 Buried in sorrow and in sin,
At hell's dark door we lay;
But we arise by grace divine,
To see a heavenly day.

3 Salvation! let the echo fly,
The spacious earth around;
While all the armies of the sky
Conspire to raise the sound.

26.

C. M.

1 JOY to the world! the Lord is come,
Let earth receive her King;

Let every heart prepare him room,
And heaven and nature sing.

2 Joy to the earth! the Saviour reigns,
Let men their songs employ, [plains,
While field and floods, rocks, hills and
Repeat the sounding joy.

3 No more let sins and sorrows grow,
Nor thorns infest the ground,
He comes to make his blessings flow
Far as the curse is found.

4 He rules the world with truth and grace,
And makes the nations prove
The glories of his righteousness,
And wonders of his love.

27.

L. M.

1 OUR Lord is risen from the dead,
Our Jesus is gone up on high;
The powers of hell are captive led,
Dragged to the portals of the sky.

2 There his triumphal chariot waits,
And angels chant the joyful lay;
Lift up your heads, ye heavenly gates,
Ye everlasting doors give way.

3 Loose all your bars of massy light,
And wide unfold the radiant scene;
He claims those mansions as his right,
Receive the King of Glory in.

4 Who is the King of Glory, who?
The Lord that all his foes o'ercame,
The world, sin, death and hell o'erthrew!
And Jesus is the conqueror's name.

28.

7s.

Value of Religion.

1 'TIS religion that can give
Sweetest pleasure while we live;
'Tis religion must supply
Solid comfort when we die.

2 After death its joys will be
Lasting as eternity;
Be the living God my friend,
Then my bliss shall never end.

29.

C. M.

1 RELIGION is the chief concern
Of mortals here below;
May I its great importance learn,
Its sovereign virtue know.

2 Religion should our thoughts engage,
Amidst our youthful bloom,
'Twill fit us for declining age,
Or for an early tomb.

3 O may my heart, by grace renew'd,
Be my Redeemer's throne,
And be my stubborn will subdued,
His government to own.

4 Let deep repentance, faith and love,
Be joined with godly fear,
And all my conversation prove
My heart to be sincere.

30.

S. M.

1 A CHARGE to keep I have,
A God to glorify;
A never-dying soul to save,
And fit it for the sky.

2 To serve the present age,
My calling to fulfill,
O may it all my powers engage
To do my Master's will.

3 Arm me with jealous care,
As in thy sight to live,

And, O! thy servant, Lord, prepare,
  A strict account to give.

4 Help me to watch and pray,
  And on thyself rely;
Assured, if I my trust betray,
  I shall forever die.

31.

C. M.

1 BEHOLD the Saviour of mankind,
  Nailed to the shameful tree;
How vast the love that him inclined
  To bleed and die for me.

2 Hark, how he groans, while nature shakes,
  And earth's strong pillars bend;
The temple's veil in sunder breaks,
  The solid marbles rend.

3 'Tis done! the precious ransom's paid;
  "Receive my soul!" he cries;
See where he bows his sacred head!
  He bows his head and dies.

4 But soon he'll break death's envious chain,
  And in full glory shine;
O Lamb of God, was ever pain,
  Was ever love like thine!

32.

8s and 7s. WASH. GLASS.

1 COME thou, everlasting Spirit,
Bring to every thankful mind,
All the Saviour's dying merit,
All his sufferings for mankind.

CHORUS.

None but Jesus, none but Jesus,
Can do helpless sinners good;
None but Jesus, none but Jesus,
Can do helpless sinners good.

2 True recorder of his passion,
Now the living fire impart;
Now reveal his great salvation,
Preach his gospel to our heart.
Chorus

3 Come, thou witness of his dying,
Come remembrancer divine,
Let us feel thy power applying
Christ to every soul and mine.
Chorus.

4 Let us groan thine inward groaning;
Look on him we pierced, and grieve;
All receive the grace atoning,
All the sprinkled blood receive.
Chorus.

33.

Canaan.

1 TOGETHER let us sweetly live,
I am bound for the land of Canaan;
In peace which none but Christ can give,
I am bound for the land of Canaan.

CHORUS.

O Canaan! bright Canaan!
I am bound for the land of Canaan;
O Canaan! it is my happy home:
I am bound for the land of Canaan.

2 There is my house not made with hands,
I am bound for the land of Canaan;
And there my Saviour waiting stands,
I am bound for the land of Canaan.
O Canaan, &c.

3 This sinful world is not my rest,
I am bound for the land of Canaan;
I long to lean on Jesus' breast,
I am bound for the land of Canaan.
O Canaan, &c.

34.

L. M.

The Poor Wayfaring Man.

1 A poor wayfaring man of grief,
Hath often crossed me on my way,

Who sued so humbly for relief,
  That I could never answer nay.
I had not power to ask his name—
Whither he went, or whence he came,
Yet there was something in his eye
That won my love, I know not why.

2 Once, when my scanty meal was spread,
  He entered—not a word he said—
Just perishing for want of bread;
  I gave him all—he blessed it—brake,
And ate, but gave me part again;
Mine was an angel's portion, then,
And while I fed with eager haste
The crust was manna to my taste.

3 I spied him where a fountain burst [gone,
  Clear from the rock—his strength was
The heedless water mocked his thirst;
  He heard it—saw it hurrying on.
I ran and raised the sufferer up;
Thrice from the stream he drained my cup,
Dipped and returned it running o'er—
I drank, and never thirsted more.

4 Stripped, wounded, beaten nigh to death,
  I found him by the highway side,

I roused his pulse, brought back his breath,
  Revived his spirit, and supplied
Wine, oil, refreshment—he was healed.
I had, myself, a wound concealed.
But from that hour forgot the smart,
And peace bound up my broken heart.

5 In prison I saw him next, condemned
  To meet a traitor's doom at morn;
The tide of lying tongues I stemmed.
  And honored him 'mid shame and scorn.
My friendship's utmost zeal to try,
He asked if I for him would die;
The flesh was weak, my blood ran chill,
But the free spirit cried, "I will."

6 Then, in a moment, to my view,
  The stranger started from disguise;
The tokens in his hands I knew,
  My Saviour stood before my eyes.
He spake, and my poor name he named,
"Of me thou hast not been ashamed;
These deeds shall thy memorial be,
Fear not, thou didst it unto me."

35.

8s & 7s.

Expostulation.

1 NOW the Saviour standeth pleading
At the sinner's bolted heart;
Now in heaven he 's interceding—
Undertaking sinners' part.

CHORUS.

Sinner, can you hate this Saviour?
Will you thrust him from your arms?
Once he died for your behaviour,
Now he calls you to his charms.

2 Sinner, hear your God and Saviour,
Hear his gracious voice to-day,
Turn from all your vain behaviour,
O, repent, return and pray.
Chorus.

3 Now he 's waiting to be gracious,
Now he stands and looks on thee,
See what kindness, love, and pity,
Shine around on you and me.
Chorus.

4 Come, for all things now are ready,
Yet there 's room for many more;

O, ye blind, ye lame and needy,
Come to wisdom's boundless store.
Chorus.

36.

P. M.

Pilgrim's Farewell.

1 FAREWELL, dear friends, I must be gone,
I have no home or stay with you;
I 'll take my staff and travel on,
Till I a better world do view.

CHORUS.

I'll march to Canaan's land,
I'll land on Canaan's shore,
Where pleasures never end,
Where troubles come no more.

2 Farewell, my friends, time rolls along,
Nor waits for mortals' care or bliss,
I leave you here and travel on,
Till I arrive where Jesus is.
I'll march, &c.

3 Farewell, my brethren in the Lord,
To you I 'm bound in cords of love,
Yet we believe his gracious word,
That soon we all shall meet above.
I'll march, &c.

4 Farewell, ye blooming sons of God,
Sore conflicts yet await for you,
Yet, dauntless, keep the heavenly road,
Till Canaan's happy land you view.
I'll march, &c.

5 Farewell, poor careless sinner, too,
It grieves my heart to leave you here;
Eternal vengeance waits for you:
O turn, and find salvation near.
I'll march, &c.

37.

C. M.

1 FATHER, I stretch my hands to thee;
No other help I know;
If thou withdraw thyself from me,
Ah whither shall I go?

2 What did thine only Son endure
Before I drew my breath!
What pain, what labor, to secure
My soul from endless death!

3 O Jesus, could I this believe,
I now should feel thy power;
Now my poor soul thou wouldst retrieve,
Nor let me wait one hour.

4 Author of faith! to thee I lift
My weary, longing eyes;
O let me now receive that gift—
My soul without it dies.

5 Surely thou canst not let me die—
O speak, and I shall live;
And here I will unwearied lie,
Till thou thy Spirit give.

6 The worst of sinners would rejoice,
Could they but see thy face;
O let me hear thy quickening voice,
And taste thy pardoning grace.

38.

C. M.

But two ways.

1 THERE is a path that leads to God—
All others go astray;
Narrow, but pleasant is the road,
And Christians love the way.

2 It leads straight through this world of sin,
And dangers must be past;
But those who boldly walk therein
Will come to heaven at last;

3 While the broad road where thousands go'
Lies near, and opens fair,

And many turn aside, I know,
To walk with sinners there.

4 But, lest my feeble steps should slide,
Or wander from thy way,
Lord, condescend to be my guide,
And I shall never stray.

39.

L. M.

The Fear of Death Removed.

1 WHY should we start, and fear to die?
What timorous worms we mortals are!
Death is the gate to endless joy,
And yet we dread to enter there.

2 The pains, the groans, the dying strife,
Fright our approaching souls away,
And we shrink back again to life,
Fond of our prison and our clay.

3 O, if my Lord would come and meet,
My soul would stretch her wings in haste—
Fly fearless through death's iron gate,
Nor feel the terrors as she passed.

4 Jesus can make a dying bed
Feel soft as downy pillows are,
While on his breast I lean my head,
And breathe my life out sweetly there.

40.

C. M.

A thought of Death and Glory.

1 MY soul, come meditate the day,
And think how near it stands,
When thou must quit this house of clay,
And fly to unknown lands.

2 O could we die with those that die,
And place us in their stead;
Then would our spirits learn to fly,
And commune with the dead.

3 Then we should see the saints above,
In their own glorious forms,
And wonder why our souls should love
To dwell with mortal worms.

4 We should almost forsake our clay
Before the summons come;
Our souls would mount and fly away,
To their eternal home.

41.

L. M.

Loving Kindness.

1 AWAKE, my soul, in joyful lays,
And sing thy great Redeemer's praise;

He justly claims a song from me—
His loving kindness, O how free!
  His loving kindness, &c.

2 He saw me ruined by the fall,
Yet loved me, notwithstanding all;
He saved me from my lost estate—
His loving kindness, O how great!
  His loving kindness, &c.

3 Though numerous hosts of mighty foes,
Though earth and hell my way oppose,
He safely leads my soul along—
His loving kindness, O how strong!
  His loving kindness, &c.

4 When trouble, like a gloomy cloud,
Has gathered thick and thundered loud,
He near my soul has always stood—
His loving kindness, O how good!
  His loving kindness, &c.

5 Often I feel my sinful heart,
Prone from my Jesus to depart;
Yet though I have him oft forgot,
His loving kindness changes not.
  His loving kindness, &c.

6 Soon shall I pass the gloomy vale—
Soon all my mortal powers must fail;
O may my last expiring breath
His loving kindness sing in death.
His loving kindness, &c.

42.

L. M. D.
Star of Bethlehem.

1 WHEN marshaled on the nightly plain,
The glittering host bestud the sky,
One star alone, of all the train,
Can fix the sinner's wandering eye.
Hark! hark! to God the chorus breaks,
From every host, from every gem;
But one alone the Saviour speaks,
It is the Star of Bethlehem.

2 Once on the raging seas I rode;
The storm was loud, the night was dark,
The ocean yawned and rudely blowed
The wind that toss'd my foundering bark.
Deep horror then my vitals froze—
Death struck, I ceased the tide to stem,
When suddenly a star arose:
It was the Star of Bethlehem.

3 It was my guide, my light, my all—
It bade my dark foreboding cease,

And thro' the storm and danger's thrall,
It led me to the port of peace.
Now safely moored—my perils o'er,
I'll sing, first in night's diadem,
Forever, and forevermore,
The Star, the Star of Bethlehem.

43.

8s & 7s. Rev. T. Jones.

The Ebenezer Hymn.

1 COME, thou fount of every blessing,
Tune my heart to sing thy grace;
Streams of mercy, never ceasing,
Call for songs of loudest praise.

CHORUS.

I will arise and go to Jesus,
He'll embrace me in his arms;
In the arms of my dear Saviour,
O there are ten thousand charms.

2 Jesus sought me when a stranger,
Wandering from the fold of God;
He, to save my soul from danger,
Interposed his precious blood.
Chorus.

3 O to grace how great a debtor,
Daily I'm constrained to be;

Let that grace, Lord, like a fetter,
Bind my wandering heart to thee.
Chorus.

4 Prone to wander, Lord, I feel it,
Prone to leave the God I love;
Here 's my heart, Lord, take and seal it,
Seal it for thy courts above.
Chorus.

44.

7s.

Child, your Father calls, Come Home.

1 BRETHREN, while we sojourn here,
Fight we must—but should not fear,
Foes we have—but we 've a friend,
One who loves us to the end.
Forward, then, with courage go,
Long we shall not dwell below,
Soon the joyful news will come :
Child, your Father calls—come home!

2 In the world a thousand snares
Lay to take us unawares—
Satan, with malicious art,
Watches each unguarded heart;
But from Satan's malice free,
Saints shall soon victorious be.

Soon the joyful news will come:
Child, your Father calls—come home!

3 But of all the foes we meet,
None so apt to turn our feet,
None betray us into sin,
Like the foes we have within.
Yet let nothing spoil your peace,
Christ will also conquer these.
Then the joyful news will come:
Child, your Father calls—come home!

45.

The Bower of Prayer.

1 TO leave my dear friends, and with neighbors to part,
And go from my home, afflicts not my heart,
Like the thought of absenting myself for a day,
From that blest retreat, where I 've chosen to pray.

2 Dear bower, where the pine and the poplar have spread,
And wove, with their branches, a roof o'er my head,

How oft have I knelt on the evergreen
there,
And poured out my soul to my Saviour
in prayer.

3 The early, shrill notes of the loved nightingale,
That dwelt in my bower, I marked as my
bell,
To call me to duty, while birds in the air,
Sang anthems of praise, as I went to
prayer.

4 How sweet were the breezes perfumed by
the pine,
The ivy, the balsam, the wild eglantine,
But sweeter, O, sweeter, superlative, were
The joys that I tasted in answer to prayer.

5 For Jesus, my Saviour, oft deigned there
to meet,
And bless, with his presence, my lowly
retreat;
Oft filled me with rapture, and blessedness there,
And gave me a foretaste of heaven in
prayer.

6 Dear bower, I must leave you and bid you adieu,
And pay my devotions in parts that are new,
Well knowing my Saviour resides everywhere,
And can in all places give answer to prayer.

46.

7s.

Christ's Reign upon Earth.

1 HASTEN, Lord, the glorious time,
When, beneath Messiah's sway,
Every nation, every clime,
Shall the gospel call obey.

2 Highest kings his power shall own,
Heathen tribes his name adore,
Satan and his host o'erthrown,
Bound in chains, shall hurt no more.

3 Then shall wars and tumults cease,
Then be banished grief and pain,
Righteousness and joy and peace,
Undisturbed shall ever reign.

47.

12s.

Awful Pomp of Judgment.

1 THE chariot, the chariot, its wheels roll
in fire,
As the Lord cometh down in the pomp of
his ire;
Lo, self-moving, it drives on its pathway
of cloud,
And the heavens with the burden of God-
head are bowed.

2 The glory, the glory, around him are
pour'd,
Mighty hosts of the angels that wait on
the Lord;
And the glorified saints and the martyrs
are there,
And there all who the palm wreaths of
victory wear.

3 The trumpet, the trumpet, the dead have
all heard;
Lo, the depths of the stone-covered char-
nel are stirred—
From the sea, from the earth, from the
south, from the north,
All the vast generations of man are come
forth.

4 The judgment, the judgment, the thrones are all set,
Where the Lamb and the white-vested elders are met;
There all flesh is at once in the sight of the Lord,
And the doom of eternity hangs on his word.

5 O mercy, O mercy, look down from above,
Great Creator, on us, thy poor children, with love;
When beneath, to the darkness, the wicked are driven,
May our justified souls find a place in heaven.

48.

The Saint's Sweet Home.

1 'MID scenes of confusion and creature complaints,
How sweet to my soul is communion with saints—
To find at the banquet of mercy there 's room,
And feel, in the presence of Jesus, at home.

CHORUS.

Home, home, sweet, sweet, home,
Receive me, dear Saviour, in glory, my home.

2 Sweet bonds that unite all the children of peace,
And thrice precious Jesus, whose love cannot cease,
Though oft from thy presence in sadness I roam,
I long to behold thee in glory at home.
Chorus.

3 I sigh from this body of sin to be free,
Which hinders my joy and communion with thee;
Though now my temptations like billows may foam,
All, all will be peace when I'm with thee at home. *Chorus.*

4 I long, dearest Lord, in thy beauties to shine,
No more as an exile in sorrow to pine,
And in thy dear image to rise from the tomb,
With glorified millions to praise thee at home. *Chorus.*

49.

S. M.

1 THE day is past and gone,
The evening shades appear,
O, may we all remember well,
The night of death draws near.

2 We lay our garments by,
Upon our beds to rest,
So death will soon disrobe us all
Of what we here possess.

3 Lord, keep us safe this night,
Secure from all our fears,
May angels guard us while we sleep,
Till morning light appears.

4 And if we early rise,
And view the unwearied sun,
May we set out to win the prize,
And after glory run.

5 And when our days are past,
And we from time remove,
O, may we in thy bosom rest—
The bosom of thy love.

50.

7s & 6s.

Missionary Hymn.

1 FROM Greenland's icy mountains,
From India's coral strand,
Where Afric's sunny fountains
Roll down their golden sand;
From many an ancient river,
From many a palmy plain,
They call us to deliver
Their land from error's chain.

2 What though the spicy breezes
Blow soft o'er Ceylon's isle;
Though every prospect pleases,
And only man is vile:
In vain with lavish kindness
The gifts of God are strewn;
The heathen in his blindness
Bows down to wood and stone.

3 Shall we, whose souls are lighted
With wisdom from on high;
Shall we to men benighted
The lamp of life deny?
Salvation, O salvation!
The joyful sound proclaim;

Till earth's remotest nation
Has learnt Messiah's name.

4 Waft—waft, ye winds, his story,
And you, ye waters, roll,
Till, like a sea of glory,
It spreads from pole to pole.
Till o'er our ransomed nature,
The Lamb for sinners slain—
Redeemer, King, Creator—
Returns in bliss to reign.

51. *O, there will be Mourning.*

1 O, THERE will be mourning,
Mourning, mourning, mourning,
O, there will be mourning
At the judgment seat of Christ.
Parents and children there will part,
Parents and children there will part,
Parents and children there will part—
Will part to meet no more.

2 O, there will be mourning, &c.
Wives and husbands there will part, &c.

3 O, there will be mourning, &c.
Brothers and sisters there will part, &c.

4 O, there will be mourning, &c.
Pastors and people there will part, &c.

5 O, there will be glory,
Glory, glory, glory,
O, there will be glory
At the judgment seat of Christ.
Saints and angels there will meet,
Saints and angels there will meet,
Saints and angels there will meet—
Will meet to part no more.

52.

8s & 7s.
Glory in the Cross.

1 WHEN the waves of life o'ertake me,
Hopes deceive, and fears annoy,
Never shall the cross forsake me;
Lo! it glows with peace and joy.

CHORUS.

Turn to the Lord, and seek salvation,
Sound the praise of his dear name;
Glory, honor, and salvation—
Christ, the Lord, is come to reign.

2 When the sun of bliss is beaming
Light and love upon my way,

From the cross the radiance streaming,
Adds more lustre to the day.
Chorus.

3 Grief and blessings, pain and pleasure,
By the cross are sanctified;
Peace is there that knows no measure,
Joys that through all time abide.
Chorus.

4 In the cross of Christ I glory,
Towering o'er the wrecks of time;
All the light of sacred story
Gathers round its head sublime.
Chorus.

53. C. M. WASH. GLASS.

The Successful Resolve.

1 COME, humble sinner, in whose breast
A thousand thoughts revolve;
Come, with your guilt and fears opprest,
And make this last resolve:—

CHORUS.

I yield, I yield, I yield!
I can hold out no more.

2 I 'll go to Jesus, tho' my sins
Have like a mountain rose,

I know his courts, I'll enter in,
Whatever may oppose.—*Chorus.*

3 Prostrate I 'll lie before his throne,
And there my guilt confess;
I 'll tell him I 'm a wretch undone,
Without his sovereign grace.
Chorus.

4 I 'll to the gracious King approach,
Whose sceptre pardon gives;
Perhaps he may command my touch,
And then the suppliant lives.
Chorus.

5 Perhaps he will admit my plea—
Perhaps will hear my prayer;
But if I perish, I will pray,
And perish only there.—*Chorus.*

6 I can but perish if I go—
I am resolved to try;
For if I stay away I know
I must forever die.—*Chorus.*

54.

The Happy Land.

1 THERE is a happy land,
Far, far away,

Where saints in glory stand,
Bright, bright as day.
O, how they sweetly sing,
Worthy is our Saviour King;
Loud let his praises ring—
Praise, praise for aye.

2 Come to that happy land,
Come, come away;
Why will ye doubting stand?
Why still delay?
O we shall happy be,
When from sin and sorrow free,
Lord, we shall live with thee—
Blest, blest for aye.

3 Bright, in that happy land,
Beams every eye;
Kept by a Father's hand,
Love cannot die.
O, then to glory run—
Be a crown and kingdom won,
And bright above the sun,
We reign for aye.

55.

P. M.

1 A FEW more days on earth to spend,
And all my toils and cares shall end;

Then I shall see my God and friend,
And praise his name on high.
There 's no more sighs and no more tears,
There 's no more pains and no more fears,
But God, and Christ, and heaven appear
Unto the ravished eye.

2 Then Oh, my soul, despond no more,
The storm of life will soon be o'er,
And I shall find the peaceful shore
Of everlasting rest.
Oh happy day, Oh joyful hour, [tower
When, freed from earth, my soul shall
Beyond the reach of Satan's power,
To be forever blest.

3 My soul anticipates the day,
I 'd joyfully the call obey,
Which summonses my soul away,
To seats prepared above.
There I shall see my Saviour's face,
And dwell in his beloved embrace,
And taste the fullness of his grace,
And sing redeeming love.

4 Though dire afflictions press me sore,
And death's dark billows roll before,

Yet still by faith I see the shore,
Beyond the rolling flood.
The heavenly Canaan sweet and fair,
Before my ravished eyes appear,
Which makes me think I 'm almost there,
In yonder bright abode.

5 To earthly cares I 'd say farewell,
And triumph over death and hell,
And go where saints and angels dwell,
To praise the Eternal Three.
I 'll join with them who 're gone before,
Who sing and shout, their sufferings o'er,
Where pain and parting are no more,
To all eternity.

6 Adieu, ye scenes of noise and show,
And all this region here below,
Where nought but disappointments grow,
A better world 's in view.
My Saviour calls, I haste away,
I would not here forever stay;
Hail, ye bright realms of endless day;
Vain world, once more adieu.

56.

1 FAREWELL, loving christian, the time is at hand,
When we must be parted from this social land;
Our several engagements do call us away,
Separation is needful and we must obey.

2 Farewell, my dear brethren, farewell for a while,
We'll soon meet again if kind providence smile;
But when we are parted and scattered abroad
We'll pray for each other when wrestling with God.

3 Farewell, faithful soldiers, you'll soon be discharged,
The war's almost over, the crown is enlarged,
With singing and praising, though Jordan may roar,
You'll enter fair Canaan, and rest on the shore.

4 Farewell, ye young converts, who've listed for war,
Sore trials await you, but Jesus is near;

Although you must travel this dark wilderness,
Your Captain 's gone before you—he 'll lead you to rest.

5 Farewell, seeking mourners, ye broken in heart,
O go to the Saviour and choose the good part,
He 's full of compassion, and mighty to save,
His arms are extended—your souls he 'll receive.

6 Farewell, careless sinners, for you I do mourn,
To think of your danger and great unconcern;
You 've heard of the judgment where all must appear,
O, there you 'll stand trembling with tormenting fear.

7 Your frolics and pastimes in which you delight,
Will serve to torment you in that dread affright;
You 'll think of the sermons that you 've heard in vain,
When hope 's gone forever, of hearing again

8 Farewell, fellow travelers! farewell all around,
Should we ne'er meet again till we wake under ground,
To meet you in glory, I give you my hand,
The Saviour to praise in a pure social band.

57.

8s, 7s & 4s.
Dismission.

1 LORD, dismiss us with thy blessing,
Fill our hearts with joy and peace;
Let us each, thy love possessing,
Triumph in redeeming grace.
O, refresh us,
Traveling through this wilderness.

2 Thanks we give, and adoration,
For thy gospel's joyful sound;
May the fruits of thy salvation,
In our hearts and lives abound,
May thy presence
With us evermore be found.

3 So whene'er the signal 's given,
Us from earth to call away,
Borne on angel's wings to heaven,
Glad to leave our cumbrous clay,

May we ready
Rise and reign in endless day.

58.

C. M.

1 AMAZING grace! how sweet the sound,
That saved a wretch like me;
I once was lost, but now am found,
Was blind—but now I see.

2 'Twas grace that taught my heart to fear,
And grace my fears relieved;
How precious did that grace appear
The hour I first believed.

3 Through many dangers, toils and snares,
I have already come;
'Tis grace that brought me safe thus far,
And grace will bring me home.

4 The Lord has promised good to me—
His word my hope secures;
He will my shield and portion be,
As long as life endures.

5 Yes, when this flesh and heart shall fail,
And mortal life shall cease,
I shall possess within the vail
A life of joy and peace.

6 The earth shall soon dissolve like snow,
  The sun forbear to shine,
But God, who called me here below,
  Will be forever mine.

59.

C. M.

1 WELL met, dear friends, in Jesus' name,
  Come let us now rejoice,
While we our Saviour's praise proclaim,
  With cheerful heart and voice.

2 In vain, dear Saviour, here we meet,
  Except thy face we see;
Thy presence makes a heaven most sweet,
  Whene'er we meet with thee.

60.

L. M.

1 BROAD is the road that leads to death,
  And thousands walk together there,
But wisdom shows a narrow path,
  With here and there a traveler.

2 Deny thyself and take thy cross,
  Is the Redeemer's great command,
Nature must count her gold but dross,
  If she would gain this heavenly land.

3 The fearful soul that tires and faints,
  And walks the ways of God no more,

Is but esteem'd almost a saint,
And makes his own destruction sure.

4 Lord, let not all my hopes be vain,
Create my heart entirely new,
Which hypocrites could ne'er attain —
Which false apostates never knew.

61.

C. M.

After Sermon.

1 FAREWELL vain world, I bid adieu,
Your glories I despise,
Your friendship I no more pursue,
Your flatteries are but lies.

2 You promise happiness in vain,
Nor can you satisfy,
Your highest pleasures turn to pain,
And all your treasures die.

3 Had I the Indies east and west,
And riches of the sea,
Without my God I could not rest,
For he is all to me.

4 Then let my soul rise far above,
By faith I'll take my wing
To the eternal realms of love,
Where saints and angels sing.

5 There's love and joy that will not waste,
  There's treasures that endure,
There's pleasures that will always last
  When time shall be no more.

62. *The dying Christian. All is well.*

1 What's this that steals, that steals away my breath,
    Is it death? Is it death?
That soon will quench, will quench this vital flame,
    Is it death? Is it death?
If this be death I soon shall be
From all my pains and sorrows free,
I shall the King of glory see;
    All is well, All is well.

2 Weep not my friends, my friends weep not for me,
    All is well, All is well,
For I am pardoned, pardoned, I am free,
    All is well, All is well,
There's not a cloud that doth arise,
To hide my Jesus from mine eyes,
I soon shall mount the upper skies,
    All is well, All is well.

3 Tune, tune your harps, your harps ye
saints in glory,
All is well, All is well,
I will rehearse, rehearse the pleasing story,
All is well, All is well.
Bright angels are from glory come,
They're round my bed, they're in my room,
They wait to waft my spirit home —
All is well, All is well.

4 Hark, hark, my Lord, my Lord and master
calls me,
All is well, All is well,
I soon shall see, shall see his face in glory,
All is well, All is well,
Farewell my friends, adieu, adieu,
I can no longer stay with you,
My glittering crown appears in view,
All is well, All is well.

5 Hail! hail! all hail, ye blood-washed
throng,
Saved by grace, Saved by grace,
I soon shall join, shall join your rapturous
song,
Saved by grace, Saved by grace,
All, all is peace and joy divine,
And heaven and glory now are mine,

O, hallelujah to the Lamb,
All is well, All is well.

63.

L. M. W. B. KIRK.

1 FROM all that dwell below the skies,
Let the Creator's praise arise,
Let the Redeemer's name be sung
Through every land, by every tongue.

2 Eternal are thy mercies, Lord,
Eternal truth attends thy word,
Thy praise shall sound from shore to shore,
Till suns shall rise and set no more.

3 Your lofty themes ye mortals bring,
In songs of praise divinely sing,
The great salvation loud proclaim,
And shout for joy the Saviour's name.

4 In every land begin the song,
To every land the strains belong,
In cheerful sounds all voices raise,
And fill the world with loudest praise.

64.

7s & 6s. WASH. GLASS.

The Sinner's Cure.

1 HOW lost was my condition,
Till Jesus made me whole;

There is but one Physician
Can cure a sin-sick soul.

CHORUS.

There is balm in Gilead,
To make the wounded whole;
There 's power enough in heaven,
To cure a sin-sick soul.

2 Next door to death he found me,
And snatch'd me from the grave,
To tell to all around me
His wond'rous power to save.
There is balm, &c.

3 The worst of all diseases,
Is light compared with sin—
On every part it seizes,
But rages most within.
There is balm, &c.

4 'Tis palsy, plague and fever,
And madness, all combined;
And none but a believer
The least relief can find.
There is balm, &c.

5 From men great skill professing,
I sought a cure to gain;

But this proved more distressing,
And added to my pain.
There is balm, &c.

6 Some said that nothing ail'd me —
Some gave me up for lost;
Thus every refuge failed me,
And all my hopes were crossed.
There is balm, &c.

7 At length this great Physician —
How matchless is his grace —
Accepted my petition,
And undertook my case.
There is balm, &c.

8 First gave me sight to view him;
For sin my eyes had seal'd —
Then bid me look unto him;
I look'd, and I was healed.
There is balm, &c.

9 A dying, risen Jesus,
Seen by the eye of faith,
At once from danger frees us,
And saves the soul from death.
There is balm, &c.

10 Come then to this Physician,
His help he 'll freely give ;
He makes no hard condition,
'Tis only look and live.
There is balm, &c.

65.

8s, 8s, 6s. THOS. GILHAM.

1 MY days, my weeks, my months, my years,
Fly rapid, like the whirling spheres
Around the steady pole;
Time, like a tide, its moment keeps,
Till I shall launch those boundless deeps
Where endless ages roll.

2 The grave is near the cradle scene,
How swift the moments pass between,
And whisper as they fly:
Unthinking man, remember this—
Thou, midst thy sublunary bliss,
Must groan, and gasp, and die.

3 Long ere the sun shall run its round
We may be buried under ground,
And there in silence rot;
Alas, one hour may close the scene,
And ere twelve months may roll between,
My name be quite forgot.

4 But shall my soul be then extinct?
Or cease to live? or cease to think?
It cannot, cannot be;
Thou, my immortal, cannot die,
What wilt thou do, or whither fly,
When death shall set thee free?

5 Will mercy then its arm extend?
Will Jesus be thy guardian friend,
And heaven thy dwelling place?
Or shall insulting fiends appear,
To drag thee down to dark despair,
Beyond the reach of grace?

6 A heaven or hell for these alone,
Beyond this mortal life are known —
There is no middle state;
To-day attend the call divine,
To-morrow may be none of thine,
Or it may be too late.

66.

P. M.

The Birth of Christ.

1 HAIL, thou blest morn, when the great Mediator,
Down from the regions of glory descends,

Shepherds, go worship the babe in the manger,
Lo! for his guide, the bright angels attend.

CHORUS.

Brightest and best of the suns of the morning,
Shine on our darkness and lend us thine aid;
Star in the east, the horizon adorning,
Guide where our infant Redeemer is laid.

2 Cold on his cradle the dewdrops are shining,
Low lies his head with the beasts of the stall;
Angels adore him in slumber reclining,
Maker, and Monarch, and Saviour of all.
Chorus.

3 Say, shall we yield him in costly devotion,
Odors of Eden and offerings divine?
Gems of the mountain and pearls of the ocean?
Myrrh from the forest and gold from the mine? *Chorus.*

4 Vainly we offer each ample oblation,
Vainly with gold would his favor secure;

Richer, by far, is the heart's adoration,
Dearer to God are the prayers of the poor.
Chorus.

67.

C. M. D. Diselms.

What Dying Worms.

1 THEE we adore, eternal name,
And humbly own to thee,
How feeble is our mortal frame!
What dying worms are we!

2 Our wasting lives grow shorter still,
As months and days increase,
And every beating pulse we tell,
Leaves but the number less.

3 The year rolls round, and steals away
The breath that first it gave;
Whate'er we do, where'er we stay,
We 're traveling to the grave.

4 Dangers stand thick thro' all the ground,
To push us to the tomb,
And fierce diseases wait around,
To hurry mortals home.

5 Great God, on what a slender thread
Hang everlasting things!

The eternal state of all the dead,
Upon life's feeble strings!

6 Infinite joy or endless woe
Attend on every breath,
And yet how unconcerned we go,
Upon the brink of death.

7 Waken, O Lord, our drowsy sense,
To walk this dangerous road,
And if our souls are hurried hence,
May they be found with God.

68.

C. M.

Mourning Friends.

1 WHY do we mourn departing friends,
Or shake at death's alarms?
'Tis but the voice that Jesus sends
To call them to his arms.

2 Are we not tending upward too,
As fast as time can move?
Nor should we wish the hours more slow,
To keep us from our love.

3 Why should we tremble to convey
Their bodies to the tomb?
There the dear flesh of Jesus lay,
And left a long perfume.

4 The graves of all his saints he bless'd,
And softened every bed;
Where should the dying members rest,
But with their dying head?

5 Thence he arose, ascending high,
And showed our feet the way;
Up to the Lord our feet shall fly
At the great rising day.

69.

8s.

Longing for Christ.

1 HOW tedious and tasteless the hours,
When Jesus no longer I see; [flowers,
Sweet prospects, sweet birds, and sweet
Have lost all their sweetness to me.
The midsummer sun shines but dim,
The fields strive in vain to look gay;
But when I am happy in him
December 's as pleasant as May.

2 His name yields the richest perfume,
And sweeter than music his voice;
His presence disperses my gloom,
And makes all within me rejoice.
I should, were he always thus nigh,
Have nothing to wish or to fear,

No mortal so happy as I—
My summer would last all the year.

3 Content with beholding his face,
My all to his pleasure resigned,
No changes of season or place
Would make any change in my mind.
While blessed with a sense of his love,
A palace a toy would appear,
And prisons would palaces prove,
If Jesus would dwell with me there.

4 Dear Lord! if indeed I am thine,
If thou art my sun and my song,
Say, why do I languish and pine?
And why are my winters so long?
O, drive these dark clouds from my sky,
Thy soul-cheering presence restore,
Or take me unto thee on high,
Where winter and clouds are no more.

70.

Weep not for Me.

1 WHEN the spark of life is waning,
Weep not for me;
When the languid eye is straining,
Weep not for me.
When the feeble pulse is ceasing,
Start not at its swift decreasing,

'Tis the fettered soul's releasing—
Weep not for me.

2 When the pangs of death assail me,
Weep not for me;
Christ is mine—he cannot fail me,
Weep not for me.
Yes, though sin and doubt endeavor
From his love my soul to sever,
Jesus is my strength forever—
Weep not for me.

71.

8s, 7s & 4s.

1 O'ER the gloomy hills of darkness,
Look, my soul—be still and gaze;
All the promises do travail
With a glorious day of grace.
Blessed jubilee,
Let thy glorious morning dawn.

2 Let the Indian, let the negro—
Let the rude barbarian see
That divine and glorious conquest
Once obtained on Calvary:
Let the gospel
Loud resound from pole to pole.

3 Kingdoms wide, that sit in darkness,
Grant them, Lord, thy glorious light;
And from eastern coast to western,
May the morning chase the night;
And redemption,
Freely purchased, win the day.

4 [May the glorious day approaching,
On their grossest darkness dawn,
And the everlasting gospel
Spread abroad thy holy name,
All the borders
Of the great Immanuel's land.]

5 Fly abroad, thou mighty gospel,
Win and conquer—never cease;
May thy lasting wide dominions
Multiply and still increase.
Sway thy sceptre,
Saviour, all the world around.

72.

C. M.

1 OF Jesus Christ I 'm not ashamed,
Although I am a child;
My soul, through grace, he has reclaimed,
By sin 'twas all defiled.

CHORUS.

I am bound for the promised land,
I am bound for the promised land!
O who will come and go with me?
I am bound for the promised land.

2 Not fourteen years have rolled away
Since first I drew my breath;
O Lord sustain my vows to-day,
And keep me firm till death.
Chorus.

3 Companions, dear, it grieves my keart
To leave you still in sin;
Farewell, farewell, I must depart,
And heavenly glories win.
Chorus.

73.

11s.

I would not live alway.

1 I WOULD not live alway: I ask not to stay,
Where storm after storm rises dark o'er the way;
The few lurid mornings that dawn on us here
Are enough for life's woes—full enough for its cheer.

2 I would not live alway, thus fettered by sin—
Temptation without, and corruption within;
E'en the rapture of pardon is mingled with fears,
And the cup of thanksgiving with penitent tears.

3 I would not live alway: no, welcome the tomb,
Since Jesus hath lain there, I dread not its gloom;
There sweet be my rest till he bid me arise
To hail him in triumph descending the skies.

4 Who, who would live alway away from his God?
Away from yon heaven—that blissful abode,
Where the rivers of pleasure flow o'er the bright plains,
And the noontide of glory eternally reigns?

5 Where the saints of all ages in harmony meet,
Their Saviour and brethren transported to greet—

While the anthems of rapture unceasingly
roll,
And the smile of the Lord is the feast of
the soul.

74.

C. M. WASH. GLASS.

The Happy Land.

1 ON Jordan's stormy banks I stand,
And cast a wishful eye,
To Canaan's fair and happy land,
Where my possessions lie.

CHORUS.

Crying victory, O victory,
O victory over death;
Crying victory, O victory,
I long to see that day.

2 O, the transporting, rapturous scene,
That rises to my sight,
Sweet fields arrayed in living green,
And rivers of delight.
Crying victory, O victory, &c.

3 All o'er those wide extended plains,
Shines one eternal day,
There God the Son forever reigns
And scatters night away.
Crying victory, O victory, &c.

4 No chilling winds nor poisonous breath,
Can reach that healthful shore,
Sickness and sorrow, pain and death,
Are felt and feared no more.
Crying victory, O victory, &c.

5 When shall I reach that happy place,
And be forever blest?
When shall I see my father's face,
And in his bosom rest?
Crying victory, O victory, &c.

6 Fill'd with delight, my raptured soul
Would here no longer stay;
Though Jordan's waves around me roll,
Fearless I'd launch away.
Crying victory, O victory, &c.

75. C. M.

1 OUR souls by love together knit,
Cemented—mix'd in one;
One hope, one heart, one mind, one voice,
'T is heaven on earth begun;
Our hearts have burned while Jesus spake,
And glow'd with sacred fire;
He stopp'd and talk'd, and fed and bless'd,
And filled the enlarged desire.

CHORUS.

A Saviour! let creation sing;
A Saviour! let all heaven ring;
He's God with us—we feel him ours,
His fullness in our souls he pours,
'Tis almost done, 't is almost o'er,
We're joining them who're gone before,
We soon shall meet to part no more.

2 We're soldiers fighting for our God,
Let trembling cowards fly;
We stand unshaken, firm and fix'd,
With Christ to live and die.
Let devils rage, and hell assail,
We'll cut our passage through;
Though foes unite and friends all fail,
We'll seize the crown we view.
Chorus.

3 The little cloud increases still—
The heavens are big with rain,
We haste to catch the teeming showers,
And all its moisture drain.
A rill, a stream, a torrent flows,
But pours a mighty flood;
Oh, sweep the nations, shake the earth,
Till all proclaim thee God.—*Chorus.*

4 And when thou mak'st thy jewels up,
And set'st thy starry crown,
When they all sparkling gems shall shine,
Proclaim'd by thee thy own,
May we, a little band of love,
Be sinners sav'd by grace,
From glory into glory chang'd,
Behold thee face to face.—*Chorus.*

76.

6s & 5s.

1 O Jesus, my Saviour,
To thee I submit,
With love and thanksgiving
Fall down at thy feet.
The sacrifice offered,
My soul, flesh and blood,
Thou art my Redeemer,
My Lord, and my God.

2 I love thee, I love thee,
I love thee, my Lord;
I love thee, my Saviour,
I love thee, my God.
I love thee, I love thee,
And that thou dost know,
But how much I love thee
I never can show.

3 I'm happy, I'm happy—
O, wond'rous account—
My joys are immortal,
I stand on the mount;
I gaze on my treasure
And long to be there,
With angels my kindred,
And Jesus my dear.

4 O Jesus, my Saviour,
In thee I am blest;
My life and my treasure,
My joy and my rest.
Thy grace is my theme,
And thy name is my song;
Thy love doth inspire
My heart and my tongue.

5 All human expressions
Are empty and vain,
They cannot unriddle
The heavenly flame.
I am sure, if the tongue
Of an angel I had,
I could not the mystery,
Completely describe.

6 O, who is like Jesus?
He's Salem's great king—
He smiles and he loves me,
He learns me to sing.
I'll praise my dear Jesus,
I love his dear name;
I'll love and I'll praise him
When the world's in a flame.

77.

My Bible.

1 MY Bible leads to glory,
My Bible leads to glory,
My Bible leads to glory,
Ye followers of the Lamb.

CHORUS.

Sing on, pray on,
Ye followers of Immanuel,
Sing on, pray on,
Ye followers of the Lamb.

2 Religion makes me happy,
Religion, &c. *Chorus.*

3 King Jesus is my captain,
King Jesus is, &c. *Chorus.*

4 I long to see my Saviour,
I long, &c. *Chorus.*

5 Then farewell, sin and sorrow,
Then farewell, &c. *Chorus.*

78.

P. M.

The Pilgrim Stranger.

1 WHITHER goest thou, pilgrim stranger,
Wandering through this gloomy vale?
Know'st thou it is full of danger,
And will not thy courage fail?

ANSWER.

No, I'm bound for the kingdom,
Will you go to glory with me?
Hallelujah, praise ye the Lamb.

2 "Pilgrim," thou dost justly call me,
Traveling through this lonely road,
But no ill shall e'er befall me
While I'm blest with such a guide.
Answer.

3 Guide unseen—but still believe me,
Jesus does my steps attend;
He'll in every strait relieve me—
He'll be with me to the end.
Answer.

4 Jordan's stream has nothing frightful,
Though its waves look dark and drear.

Death itself will be delightful,
Jesus will be with me there.
Answer.

79.

L. M.
Prayer for the Spirit.

1 AT anchor laid, remote from home,
Toiling I cry—sweet Spirit, come;
Celestial breeze, no longer stay,
But swell my sails and speed my way.

2 Fain would I mount, fain would I glow,
And loose my cable from below,
But I can only spread my sail,
Thou, thou must breathe the auspicious gale.

80.

C. M.
Remember me.

1 JESUS, my advocate on high,
I yield myself to thee,
While thou art sitting on thy throne,
O Lord, remember me.

CHORUS.

Remember me, remember me,
Dear Lord, remember me.

2 I own I'm guilty—own I'm vile,
Yet thy salvation's free;

Then in thy all abounding grace,
O Lord, remember me.— *Chorus.*

3 Howe'er forsaken or distressed,
Howe'er oppressed I be,
Howe'er afflicted here on earth,
Do thou remember me.— *Chorus.*

4 And when I close my eyes in death,
And creature helps all flee,
Then, O my great Redeemer—God,
I pray remember me. *Chorus.*

81.

11s.

Heavenly Contemplation.

1 FROM gloomy dejection my thoughts mount the sky,
And realms ever peaceful transported descry,
There joys ever blooming enrapture the soul,
And rivers of pleasure unceasingly roll.

2 If such be my portion, why should I complain ?
Why cherish despondence ? why sadness retain ?
Is sorrow, then, meet for an heir of the skies,
Who shortly to blessings unbounded shall rise?

3 No longer I'll murmur, no longer repine,
But joy mid all troubles, since heaven is mine;
Then deep in oblivion be sunk every fear—
Be erased from my bosom each trace of despair.

4 How glorious the scheme that grace doth enhance,
Our hopes to enliven, our bliss to advance;
It fills me with transport, my joys overflow,
Too big for expression, ecstatic they grow.

5 O aid me, ye angels, its wonders to tell,
Encompass the theme, in full symphony dwell;
But still it enlarges — no angel can scan
The scheme of redemption — the wonderful plan.

82.

C. M. WASH. GLASS.

1 AM I a soldier of the cross?
A follower of the Lamb?
And shall I fear to own his cause,
Or blush to speak his name?

CHORUS.

O, the Lamb, the loving Lamb,
The Lamb on Calvary;

The Lamb that was slain,
But liveth again,
To intercede for me.

2 Must I be carried to the skies,
On flowery beds of ease,
While others fought to win the prize,
And sailed through bloody seas?
Chorus.

3 Are there no foes for me to face?
Must I not stem the flood?
Is this vile world a friend to grace
To help me on to God?
Chorus.

4 Sure, I must fight if I would reign,
Increase my courage, Lord;
I'll bear the toil — endure the pain,
Supported by thy word.
Chorus.

5 Thy saints in all this glorious war
Shall conquer, though they die;
They see the triumph from afar,
And seize it with their eye.
Chorus.

6 When that illustrious day shall rise,
And all thy armies shine
In robes of victory through the skies,
The glory shall be thine.
Chorus.

83.

L. M.
The Mercy Seat.

1 FROM every stormy wind that blows,
From every swelling tide of woes,
There is a calm, a sure retreat —
'T is found beneath the mercy-seat.

2 There is a place where Jesus sheds
The oil of gladness on our heads —
A place of all on earth most sweet;
It is the blood-bought mercy-seat.

3 There is a scene where spirits blend,
Where friend holds fellowship with friend;
Though sundered far, by faith they meet
Around one common mercy-seat.

4 There, there, on eagle wings we soar,
And sin and sense molest no more;
And heaven comes down our souls to greet,
And glory crowns the mercy-seat.

84.

C. M.

Hinder me not.

1 IN all my Lord's appointed ways,
My journey I'll pursue;
Hinder me not, ye much loved saints,
For I must go with you.

2 Through floods and flames—if Jesus lead,
I'll follow where he goes;
Hinder me not, shall be my cry,
Though earth and hell oppose.

3 Stay, says the world, and taste a while,
My every pleasant sweet;
Hinder me not, my soul replies,
Because the way is great.

4 Stay, Satan my old master cries,
Or force shall thee detain;
Hinder me not, I will be gone,
My God hath broke my chain.

5 Through duty, and through trials too,
I'll go at his command;
Hinder me not, for I am bound
To my Immanuel's land.

6 And when my Saviour calls me home,
Still this my cry shall be,

Hinder me not — come, welcome death,
I'll gladly go with thee.

85.

8s & 6s. Rev. T. Jones.

1 COME on, my partners in distress,
My comrades through the wilderness,
Who still your bodies feel,
Awhile forget your griefs and fears,
And look beyond this vale of tears,
To that celestial hill.

2 Beyond the bounds of time and space,
Look forward to that heavenly place—
The saints' secure abode;
On faith's strong eagle pinions rise,
And force your passage to the skies,
And scale the mount of God.

3 Who suffer with our Master here,
We shall before his face appear,
And by his side sit down;
To patient faith the prize is sure,
And all that to the end endure
The cross, shall wear the crown.

4 Thrice blessed bliss — inspiring hope,
It lifts the fainting spirits up,
It brings to life the dead.

Our conflicts here shall soon be past,
And you and I ascend at last,
Triumphant with our head.

86.

6s & 5s.

O Jesus, my Savior.

1 O Jesus, my Saviour, I know thou art mine,
For thee all the pleasures of life I'll resign,
Of objects most pleasing I love thee the best,
Without thee I'm wretched, but with thee I'm blest.

2 Thou art my rich treasure, my joy and my love,
No richer's possessed by the angels above;
For thee all the pleasures of sense I'll forego,
And wander a pilgrim distressed below.

3 Thy Spirit first taught me to know I was blind—
Then taught me the way of salvation to find,
And when I was sinking in darkest despair,
My Saviour relieved me, and bade me not fear.

4 Though poor and despised, by faith I now stand,
Upheld and supported by heaven's kind hand;
In Jesus supported, I'll praise his dear name,
Regardless of censure, of praise or of blame.

5 I find him in singing, I find him in prayer;
In sweet meditation he always is near—
My constant companion, O may we not part;
All glory to Jesus, he dwells in my heart.

6 If ever I lov'd, sure I love thee, my Lord;
I love thy dear people, thy ways and thy word;
I love all creation—I love sinners too,
Since Jesus has died to redeem them from woe.

7 When millions of ages my soul shall employ,
In praising my Saviour, my life and my joy,
The glorified angels and spirits around,
Will all be delighted to join the glad sound.

87.

P. M. REV. T. JONES.

1 HOW happy are they
Who their Saviour obey,
And whose treasures are laid up above;

Tongue cannot express
The sweet comfort and peace
Of a soul in its earliest love.

2 That comfort was mine,
When the favor divine,
I first found in the blood of the Lamb;
When my heart it believed,
What a joy I received,
What a heaven in Jesus's name.

3 'T was a heaven below,
My Redeemer to know,
And the angels could do nothing more
Than to fall at his feet
And the story repeat,
And the Saviour of sinners adore.

4 Jesus, all the day long,
Was my joy and my song,
Oh, that more his salvation might see;
He hath lov'd me, I cried,
He hath suffered and died,
To redeem such a rebel as me.

5 On the wings of his love
I was carried above
All sin and temptation and pain,

I could not believe
That I ever should grieve,
That I ever should suffer again.

6 Oh, the rapturous height
Of that holy delight,
Which I felt in the life-giving blood,
Of the Saviour possess'd
I was perfectly bless'd,
Overwhelm'd in the goodness of God.

7 Now, my remnant of days
Would I spend in his praise,
Who hath died my poor soul to redeem;
Whether many or few,
All my years are his due,
May they all be devoted to him.

8 What a mercy is this,
What a heaven of bliss,
How unspeakably happy am I;
Gathered into the fold,
With believers enroll'd,
With believers to live and to die.

9 Lo! the day 's drawing nigh,
When, my soul, thou shalt fly
To where thy salvation began;

Where the Three and the One,
Father, Spirit, and Son,
Laid the scheme of redemption for man.

88.

11s. WASH. GLASS.

Precious Promises.

1 HOW firm a foundation, ye saints of the Lord,
Is laid for your faith in his excellent word;
What more can he say, than to you he hath said,
Ye who unto Jesus for refuge have fled?

CHORUS.

Hallelujah, hallelujah,
Hallelujah to God,
For he hath redeemed us
By his own precious blood.

2 In every condition, in sickness, in health,
In poverty's vale, or abounding in wealth,
At home and abroad, on the land, on the sea,
As thy days may demand, shall thy strength ever be. *Chorus.*

3 Fear not, I am with thee, O, be not dismayed;
I, I am thy God, and will still give thee aid;

I 'll strengthen thee, help thee, and cause
thee to stand,
Upheld by my righteous, omnipotent hand.
Chorus.

4 When through the deep waters I call thee
to go,
The rivers of sorrow shall not thee o'erflow,
For I will be with thee, thy troubles to bless,
And sanctify to thee thy deepest distress.
Chorus.

5 When through fiery trials thy pathway
shall lie,
My grace, all-sufficient, shall be thy supply,
The flame shall not hurt thee, I only design,
Thy dross to consume, and thy gold to refine.
Chorus.

6 The soul that on Jesus hath lean'd for
repose,
I will not, I will not desert to his foes,
That soul, though all hell should endeavor
to shake,
I'll never, no never, no never forsake.
Chorus.

89.

8s, 5s, 7s, & 4s.
No Pleasures Here.

1 I HAVE sought round this verdant earth,
For unfading joy;
I have tried every source of mirth,
But all, all will cloy;
Lord, bestow on me,
Grace to set my spirit free,
Thine the praise shall be,
Mine, mine the joy.

2 I have wandered in mazes dark,
Of doubt and distress;
I have had not a kindling spark,
My spirit to bless.
Cheerless unbelief,
Fill'd my lab'ring soul with grief;
What shall give relief,
What shall give peace?

3 I then turned to the gospel, Lord,
From folly away,
I then trusted thy holy word,
That taught me to pray.
Here I found relief,
Here my weary soul found rest,
Hope of endless bliss,
Eternal day.

4 I will praise now my heavenly King,
I 'll praise and adore;
I 'll the heart's richest tribute bring,
To thee, God of power.
And in heaven above,
Saved by thy redeeming love,
Loud the strains shall move,
Forevermore.

90.

11s.

The House of the Lord.

1 YOU may sing of the beauty of mountains and glen,
Of the silvery streamlets and flowers of the vale;
But the place most delightful this earth can afford,
Is the place of devotion—the house of the Lord.

2 You may boast of the sweetness of day's early dawn,
Of the sky's softening graces, when day has just gone;
But there 's no other season or time can compare
With the hour of devotion—the season of prayer.

3 You may value the friendships of youth
and of age,
And select for your comrades the noble and
sage,
But the friends that most cheer me on life's
rugged road,
Are the friends of my Master—the children
of God.

4 You may talk of your prospects of fame
or of wealth,
And the hopes that oft flatter the favorites
of health;
But the hope of bright glory—of heavenly
bliss—
Take away every other, and give me but
this.

5 Ever hail, blessed temple, abode of my
Lord,
I will turn to thee often to hear from his
word;
I will walk to thy altar with those that I
love,
And rejoice in the prospect revealed from
above.

91.

11s & 8s.

The Glory of Christ.

1 O THOU in whose presence my soul takes delight,
On whom in affliction I call,
My comfort by day and my song in the night,
My hope, my salvation, my all.

2 Where dost thou at noon-tide resort with thy sheep,
To feed on the pastures of love?
Say, why in the valley of death should I weep,
Or alone in the wilderness rove?

3 O why should I wander an alien from thee,
Or cry in the desert for bread!
Thy foes will rejoice when my sorrows they see,
And smile at the tears I have shed.

4 Ye daughters of Zion declare, have ye seen
The star that on Israel shone?
Say if in your tents my beloved has been,
And where with his flock he has gone.

5 This is my beloved—his form is divine,
His vestments shed odors around;
The locks on his head are as grapes on the vine,
When autumn with plenty is crowned.

6 His voice, as the sound of the dulcimer sweet,
Is heard through the shadow of death;
The cedars of Lebanon bow at his feet—
The air is perfumed with his breath.

7 His lips, as a fountain of righteousness, flow,
To water the gardens of grace;
From which their salvation the Gentiles shall know,
And bask in the smiles of his face.

8 He looks, and ten thousands of angels rejoice,
And myriads wait for his word;
He speaks! and eternity, filled with his voice,
Reëchoes the praise of the Lord.

92.

C. M.

1 SIN hath a thousand treacherous arts,
To practice on the mind;
With flattering looks she tempts our hearts,
But leaves a sting behind.

2 With names of virtue she deceives
The aged and the young,
And while the heedless wretch believes,
She makes his fetters strong.

3 She pleads for all the joys she brings,
And gives a fair pretence;
But cheats the soul of heavenly things,
And chains it down to sense.

4 So on a tree divinely fair,
Grew the forbidden food;
Our mother took the poison there,
And tainted all her blood.

93.

P. M.
Zion.

1 ARISE and shine, O Zion fair—
Behold thy light is come;
Thy glorious conquering king is near,
To take his exiles home:

The trumpet sounding through the sky,
  To set poor sinners free;
The day of wonder now is nigh—
  The year of jubilee.

2 Ye heralds blow your trumpets loud,
  The earth must know her doom;
Go spread the news from pole to pole—
  Behold, the Judge is come!
Blow out the sun, burn up the earth!
  Consume the rolling flood;
While every star shall disappear,
  Go turn the moon to blood!

3 Arise, ye nations under ground—
  Before the Judge appear;
All tongues and languages shall come,
  Their final doom to hear.
King Jesus, on his dazzling throne,
  Ten thousand angels round,
And Gabriel, with a silver trump,
  Echoes the awful sound.

4 The glorious news of gospel grace,
  To sinners now is o'er;
The trump in Zion now is still,
  And to be heard no more:

The watchmen all have left their walls,
And with their flocks above,
On Canaan's peaceful shore they sing,
And shout redeeming love.

94.

C. M.

A Breeze of Heavenly Love.

1 O FOR a breeze of heavenly love,
To waft my soul away,
To the celestial world above,
Where pleasures ne'er decay.

2 Eternal Spirit, deign to be
My pilot here below;
To steer through life's tempestuous sea,
Where stormy winds do blow.

3 From rocks of pride on either hand,
From quicksands of despair,
O guide me safe to Canaan's land,
Through every latent snare.

4 Anchor me in that port above,
On that celestial shore
Where dashing billows never move,
Where tempests never roar.

95.

P. M.

The Love of God.

1 O how charming, O how charming,
Is the radiant band of music, music, music,
music,
O, how charming is the radiant band
Of music, playing through the air;
Angelic armies tune their harps,
Angelic armies tune their harps,
Enraptured spirits play their parts,
Angelic armies tune their harps—
Shout! Shout! the great Messiah is come to
reign.

2 Gabriel descending, Gabriel descending,
Brings the joyful news; O joyful, joyful,
joyful, joyful—
Brings the joyful news of our Redeemer's
birth;
The great Messiah 's come to earth.
Good will to men I now proclaim—
Good will to men I now proclaim,
The Saviour 's born in Bethlehem;
Good will to men I now proclaim—
Shout! Shout! the king of glory is come
to reign.

3 See his star arising, See his star arising,
In the eastern sky, now rising, rising, rising,
rising,
See his star arising in the eastern sky—
The day-spring opening from on high.
The types and shadows flee away,
The types and shadows flee away,
And now begins the gospel day,
The types and shadows flee away—
Shout! Shout! the king of glory is come
to reign.

4 Shepherds adore him, wise men have
found him—
Glory be to God; O glory, glory, glory,
glory;
Wise men have found him by the rising star,
And come to worship him afar:
Their golden gifts they now present—
Their golden gifts they now present,
And spices of the sweetest scent;
Their golden gifts they now present—
Shout! Shout! the king of glory is come
to reign.

5 Jews and Gentiles join in concert
To praise their infant king; O praise him,
praise him, praise him, praise,

Jews and Gentiles praise their infant king,
And loud hosannas sweetly sing.
  With Gabriel and the shining host—
  With Gabriel and the shining host,
  Praise Father, Son and Holy Ghost;
  With Gabriel and the shining host—
Shout! Shout! the king of glory is come to reign.

6 I am happy, I am happy—
Glory be to God; O glory, glory, glory, glory,
I am happy—glory be to God,
My soul's on flame for the realms above;
  I feel the bliss his wounds impart—
  I feel the bliss his wounds impart,
  I find my Saviour in my heart,
  I feel the bliss his wounds impart—
Shout! Shout! the king of glory is come to reign.

7 Reign, reign, sweet Jesus, reign within and round us,
By the Holy Spirit, holy, holy, holy, holy,
By the Holy Spirit keep us in the way,
That we may shout as we sing and pray.
  With all the saints that have gone home

With all the saints that have gone home,
Unite to sing redeeming love;
With all the saints that have gone home,
To sing, to sing hallelujahs around the throne.

96.

C. M.

Our glorious home in Heaven.

1 AFTER we list the seraphs' lays,
And catch their raptured strains,
And dimly through the glass of faith
Behold the heavenly plains—

CHORUS.

Then let us on to our home above,
Our glorious home in heaven—
Then let us on to our home above,
Our glorious home in heaven.

2 The friends who love, may love no more,
Or the life-chord frail be riven,
But one who'll neither change nor die,
Is waiting us in heaven.—*Chorus.*

3 On earth do bitter fountains gush,
And fading flow'rets blow—
In heaven, undying fruits are borne,
And taintless waters flow.—*Chorus.*

4 The wealth of earth must vanish all,
Before the death-dimmed eye;
Then let us strive, with tireless aim,
For wealth above the sky.— *Chorus.*

97.

L. M.

The Robe of Righteousness.

1 FAST by the river's side, that flowed
Between the living and the dead—
Rocked by the storm that fiercely blowed,
The dark long night in sleep I laid.
I dreamed my final hour drew nigh—
I saw Death's angel standing there;
I heard at last the summon-cry,
That bade my trembling soul prepare.

2 Quick springing from my couch, I seized
The robe of righteousness I'd wrought,
Of alms-deeds, prayers and tears—well pleased;
'Twould prove a sheltering garb, I thought.
Changed in the twinkling of an eye,
A mirror vast, earth, sky, became;
It showed my robe, and I could lie
Down in the lowest dust, for shame.

3 Sin-soiled and loathsome grown—I knew
How selfish every act had been,

And could but with abhorrence view
The very tears I'd shed for sin.
In tattered fragments, parting wide,
Fold after fold it dropped—the whole—
Till not a shred was left to hide
My sin-stained, vile and trembling soul.

4 Death called again: I dared not go;
I had no vesture—none would loan;
I shuddered on the verge, and lo!
My Saviour offered me his own.
Wrapped in its ample breadth, my cure
Was wrought at once; my fears were gone;
Grown into Christ, the promise sure
Was mine—the crown of glory won.

98.

P. M.

The Indian Hymn.

1 IN de dark woods, no Indian nigh,
Den me look Heb'n, and send up cry,
Upon my knee so low;
But God on high, in shiny place,
See me at night wid teary face—
De priest he tell me so.

2 God send he angel, take um care,
He come he self and hear um prayer,

(If Indian heart do pray ;)
He see me now, he know me here,
He say poor Indian neber fear,
Me wid you night and day.

3 So me lub God wid inside heart ;
He fight for me, he take um part,
He save um life before ;
God hear poor Indian in de wood,
So me lub him and dat be good ;
Me pray him two times more.*

99.

L. M.

God the Sinner's Friend.

1 HE dies: the friend of sinners dies !
Lo, Salem's daughters weep around ;
A solemn darkness veils the skies,
A sudden trembling shakes the ground.

2 Come saints and drop a tear or two,
For him who groaned beneath your load,
He shed a thousand drops for you —
A thousand drops of richer blood.

3 Here's love and grief beyond degree,
The Lord of glory dies for men ;

*Meaning twice as often as formerly.

But lo! what sudden joys we see —
Jesus, the dead, revives again.

4 The rising God forsakes the tomb;
Up to his Father's courts he flies:
Cherubic legions guard him home,
And shout him welcome to the skies.

5 Break off your tears, ye saints, and tell
How high our great deliverer reigns;
See how he spoil'd the hosts of hell,
And led the monster, death, in chains.

6 Say, live forever, wond'rous King,
Born to redeem, and strong to save;
Then ask the monster: Where's thy sting?
And where's thy victory, boasting grave?

100.

L. M.

1 YOUNG people all, attention give,
While I address you in God's name;
You who in sin and folly live,
Come hear the counsel of a friend:
I've sought for bliss in glittering toys,
I've ranged th' alluring scenes of life,
But never found substantial joys
Until I heard my Saviour's voice.

2 He spake at once my sins forgiven,
And took my load of guilt away;
He gave me glory, peace and heaven,
And thus I found the good old way.
And now with trembling sense I view
Your awful state, unthinking youth,
While death eternal waits for you,
Who slight the force of gospel truth.

3 Youth, like the spring, will soon be gone,
By fleeting time, or conquering death;
Your morning sun may set at noon,
For God may soon demand your breath.
Your sparkling eyes and blooming cheeks
Must wither like the blasted rose;
The coffin, earth, and winding sheet,
Must soon your active limbs enclose.

4 Ye heedless ones, who wildly stroll,
The grave must soon become your bed,
There darkness reigns and vapors move
In solemn silence round your head:
Your friends will pass the lonesome place,
And with a sigh, move slow along,
Still gazing at those spires of grass
Which will be o'er your bodies grown.

5 But, oh! the soul where vengeance reigns,
  It sinks in groans and ceaseless cries;
It moves amidst the burning flames,
  In boundless woes and agonies.
There swallowed up in blackest night,
  Where devils dwell and thunders roar,
To sink in keen despair and guilt,
  When thousand, thousand years are o'er.

6 Oh, thoughtless youth, this is the state
  Of all who do free grace abuse;
And soon with you 'twill be too late
  The way of life in Christ to choose.
Come, lay your carnal weapons by,
  No longer fight against your Lord,
And with my message now comply,
  And heaven shall be your great reward.

101.

C. M.

The Blood of Christ.

1 THERE is a fountain filled with blood,
  Drawn from Immanuel's veins;
And sinners, plunged beneath that flood,
  Lose all their guilty stains.

2 The dying thief rejoiced to see
  That fountain in his day;

And there would I, though vile as he,
  Wash all my sins away.

3 Dear, dying Lamb, thy precious blood
  Shall never lose its power,
Till all the ransomed church of God
  Be saved to sin no more.

4 E'er since by faith I saw the stream
  Thy flowing wounds supply,
Redeeming love has been my theme,
  And shall be, till I die.

5 Then, in a nobler, sweeter song,
  I'll sing thy power to save,
When this poor lisping, stamm'ring tongue,
  Lies silent in the grave.

6 Lord, I believe thou hast prepared—
  Unworthy, though I be—
For me a blood-bought, free reward—
  A golden harp for me.

7 'Tis strung and tuned for endless years,
  And formed by power divine,
To sound in God the Father's ears,
  No other name but thine.

102.

P. M. Rev. T. Jones.

The Gospel Trumpet.

1 ONE day as I was walking along the lonesome road,
My Saviour came unto me and fill'd my heart with love;
He chose me for his watchman, to blow the trumpet loud,
To cheer the weak believers and to invite the crowd.

2 The cross it being heavy, I then was in my youth,
Oh, how shall I be able to speak the words of truth?
But Christ said, I'll be with you, with you it shall go well,
Go blow the gospel trumpet, and do your Master's will.

3 I said unto my Saviour, my talents are but small,
Perhaps they will not hear me if on them I do call;
Well if they do not hear you, with you it shall go well,

Go blow the gospel trumpet while they go
down to hell.

4 Those blessed words of Jesus caused me
to cry and weep,
My conscience spake of Jonah, how he lay
in the deep;
I took the cross upon me, I then began to
blow,
I 'll blow the gospel trumpet, — I 'll blow
where'er I go.

5 Come all ye blood bought partners, on
you I call this day,
Fall at the feet of Jesus, and then begin to
pray;
But if you do refuse it, and disobey the call,
I 'll blow the gospel trumpet, while you go
down to hell.

6 Behold the blood of Jesus, spilled on
Mount Calvary!
Look up by faith and view him, and he will
set you free;
Sinners, if you refuse it, and disobey the
Lord,
I 'll blow the gospel trumpet, and clear me
of your blood.

103.

C. M.

Jerusalem.

1 JERUSALEM, my happy home,
O, how I long for thee;
When will my sorrows have an end?
Thy joys when shall I see?

CHORUS.

O dear Jesus, O how long
Have I on earth to stay?
Roll around the wheels of time,
And bring the promised day.

2 Thy walls are all of precious stone,
Most glorious to behold;
Thy gates are richly set with pearl,
Thy streets are paved with gold.
Chorus.

3 If heaven be thus, O glorious Lord,
Why should I stray from thence;
What folly 'tis that I should dread
To die and go from hence.—*Chorus.*

4 Reach down, reach down thine arm of grace,
And cause me to ascend,

Where congregations ne'er break up,
And Sabbaths have no end.—*Chorus.*

5 Jesus, my love, to glory 's gone,
Him will I go and see,
And all my brethren here below
Will soon come after me.—*Chorus.*

6 My friends, I bid you all adieu,
I leave you in God's care;
And if I never more see you,
Go on—I 'll meet you there.
Chorus.

7 There we shall meet, and no more part,
And heaven shall ring with praise,
While Jesus' love, in every heart,
Shall tune the song free grace.
Chorus.

8 When we 've been there ten thousand years,
Bright shining as the sun,
We 've no less days to sing God's praise,
Than when we first begun.—*Chorus.*

104.

C. M.

Death.

1 THERE is a land of pure delight,
Where saints immortal reign;
Infinite day excludes the night,
And pleasures banish pain.

2 There everlasting spring abides,
And never-withering flowers;
Death, like a narrow sea, divides
This heavenly land from ours.

3 Sweet fields beyond the swelling flood,
Stand dressed in living green;
So to the Jews old Canaan stood,
While Jordan rolled between.

4 [But tim'rous mortals start and shrink,
To cross this narrow sea,
A d linger shivering on the brink,
And fear to launch away.]

5 O, could we make our doubts remove,
Those gloomy doubts that rise,
And see the Canaan that we love,
With unbeclouded eyes;

6 Could we but climb where Moses stood,
And view the landscape o'er,
Not Jordan's stream, nor death's cold flood,
Should fright us from the shore.

105.

C. M.

Heaven begun on Earth.

1 HOW happy every child of grace,
Who knows his sins forgiven!
This earth, he cries, is not my place:
I seek my place in heaven.

2 A country far from mortal sight—
Yet O, by faith I see
The land of rest—the saints' delight—
The heaven prepared for me.

3 O, what a blessed hope is ours,
While here on earth we stay;
We more than taste the heavenly powers,
And antedate that day.

4 We feel the resurrection near—
Our life in Christ concealed,
And with his glorious presence here,
Our earthen vessels filled.

5 O would he more of heaven bestow,
And let the vessels break,
And let our ransomed spirits go,
To grasp the God we seek:

6 In rapturous awe on him to gaze,
Who bought the right for me,
And shout and wonder at his grace,
To all eternity.

106. *Death.* S. M.

1 AND must this body die,
This well wrought frame decay?
And must these active limbs of mine
Lie mouldering in the clay?

2 Corruption, earth, and worms,
Shall but refine this flesh,
Till my triumphant spirit comes,
To put it on afresh.

3 God, my Redeemer, lives,
And ever from the skies,
Looks down and watches all my dust,
Till he shall bid it rise.

4 Arrayed in glorious grace,
Shall these vile bodies shine,

And every shape and every face,
Be heavenly and divine.

5 These lively hopes we owe,
Lord, to thy dying love;
O may we bless thy grace below,
And sing thy grace above.

6 Saviour! accept the praise
Of these our humble songs,
Till tunes of nobler sounds we raise,
With our immortal tongues.

107.

WASH. GLASS.

Prayer, Sweet Prayer.

1 WHEN torn is the bosom by sorrow or care,
Be it ever so simple, there's nothing like prayer;
It eases, soothes, softens, subdues, yet sustains —
Gives vigor to hope, and puts passion in chains.

CHORUS.

Prayer, prayer, O sweet prayer,
Be it ever so simple, there's nothing like prayer.

2 When far from the friends we hold dearest, we part,
What fond recollections still cling to the heart;
Past converse, past scenes, past enjoyments are there —
O, how hurtfully pleasing till hallowed by prayer. *Chorus.*

3 When pleasure would woo us from piety's arms —
The siren sings sweetly, or silently charms,
We listen, love, loiter — are caught in the snare —
But looking to Jesus, we conquer by prayer. *Chorus.*

4 While strangers to prayer, we are strangers to bliss —
Heaven pours its full streams through no medium but this;
And till we the seraph's full ecstacy share,
Our chalice of joy must be guarded by prayer. *Chorus.*

108.

P. M.

The old Ship of Zion.

1 WHAT ship is this, that shall take us all home?
O glory, hallelujah!
What ship is this, that shall take us all home?
O glory, hallelujah!
'T is the old ship of Zion, hallelujah!
'T is the old ship of Zion, hallelujah!

2 Do you think she will be able to take us all home?
O glory, hallelujah!
Do you think she will be able to take us all home?
O glory, hallelujah!
King Jesus is her captain, hallelujah!
King Jesus is her captain, hallelujah!

3 She has landed many thousands, and will land as many more,
O glory, hallelujah!
She has landed many thousands, and will land as many more,
O glory, hallelujah!
She will land us in the kingdom, hallelujah!
She will land us in the kingdom, hallelujah!

4 The timbers they are good, and the sails are spread,
O glory, hallelujah!
The timbers they are good, and the sails are spread,
O glory, hallelujah!
She is built for rapid sailing, hallelujah!
She is built for rapid sailing, hallelujah l

5 What makes her sail so fast and free?
O glory, hallelujah!
What makes her sail so fast and free?
O glory, hallelujah!
'T is a pleasant gale for glory, hallelujah!
'T is a pleasant gale for glory, hallelujah!

6 What kind of freight has she got on board?
O glory, hallelujah!
What kind of freight has she got on board?
What kind of freight has she got on board?
O glory, hallelujah!
Souls who are converted, hallelujah!
Souls who are converted, hallelujah!

7 Come on board, come on board, and let us travel home,
O glory, hallelujah!

Come on board, come on board, and let us travel home,
O glory, hallelujah !
We are going home to glory, hallelujah !
We are going home to glory, hallelujah !

8 A few more beating winds and rains,
O glory, hallelujah !
A few more beating winds and rains,
O glory, hallelujah !
And the voyage will be over, hallelujah !
And the voyage will be over, hallelujah

9 We soon shall reach that happy shore,
O glory, hallelujah !
We soon shall reach that happy shore,
O glory, hallelujah !
And meet our friends in heaven, hallelujah !
And meet our friends in heaven, hallelujah !

10 The joyful sailors then will sing,
O glory, hallelujah !
The joyful sailors then will sing,
O glory, hallellujah !
Our dangers now are over, hallelujah !
Our dangers now are over, hallelujah !

109.

8s & 4s. REV. T. JONES.

The Sonnet.

1 WHEN for eternal worlds we steer,
And seas are calm, and skies are clear,
And faith in lively exercise,
And distant hills of Canaan rise—
The soul for joy then claps her wings,
And loud her lovely sonnet sings:
Vain world, adieu.

2 With cheerful hope, her eyes explore
Each landmark on the distant shore,
The tree of life—the pastures green,
The golden streets—the crystal stream;
Again for joy she claps her wings,
And loud her lovely sonnet sings:
Vain world, adieu.

3 The nearer still she draws to land,
More eager all her powers expand:
With steady helm and free bent sail,
Her anchor drops within the vail;
Again for joy she claps her wings,
And her celestial sonnet sings:
I'm going home.

4 Now safely moored, no storm I fear,
My God, my Christ, my heaven is here,

And all the joys of Paradise,
In holiness and beauty rise;
'Tis now the soul, with folded wings,
Her thrilling notes of joy shall sing:
Glory to God.

110.

P. M.

Give me Jesus.

1 WHILE wandering to and fro,
In this wide world of woe,
Where streams of sorrow flow—
Give me Jesus.

CHORUS.

Give me Jesus, give me Jesus!
You may have all this world: give me Jesus.

2 When tears o'erflow mine eye,
When pressed with grief I sigh,
Still this shall be my cry—
Give me Jesus.—*Chorus.*

3 When to the mercy seat
I go my Lord to meet,
My heart shall still repeat—
Give me Jesus.—*Chorus.*

4 And when my faith is tried,
In him will I confide,
And cry, whate'er betide—
Give me Jesus.—*Chorus.*

5 Tho' wealth and friends should fail,
And foes my soul assail,
Through him I shall prevail—
Give me Jesus.—*Chorus.*

6 And when my toils are o'er—
When nearing Jordan's shore,
I 'll sing, as up I soar—
Give me Jesus.—*Chorus.*

7 When at the judgment seat,
Earth's countless millions meet,
The choice will then be sweet—
Give me Jesus.—*Chorus.*

8 When time shall cease to be—
When heaven and earth shall flee,
I 'll sing eternally—
Give me Jesus.—*Chorus.*

111.

The Happy Convert.

1 COME, ye that fear the Lord, unto me,
unto me,
Come, ye that fear the Lord, unto me;
I 've something good to say
About the narrow way,
For Christ, the other day, saved my soul.

2 He gave me first to see what I was, what
I was,
He gave me first to see what I was;
He gave me first to see
My guilt and misery,
And then he set me free—bless his name.

3 My old companions said he's undone, he's
undone,
My old companions said he's undone;
My old companions said
He 's surely going mad;
But Jesus makes me glad—bless his name.

4 O if they did but know what I feel, what
I feel,
O if they did but know what I feel;
Had they but eyes to see
Their guilt and misery,
They'd be as mad as me—I believe.

5 Some said he 'll soon give o'er—you shall
see, you shall see,
Some said he 'll soon give o'er, you shall
see;
Some time has passed away
Since I began to pray,
And I feel the Lord to-day—bless his
name.

6 And now I 'm going home to the Lord,
to the Lord,
And now I 'm going home to the Lord;
And now I'm going home—
Poor sinner wilt thou come,
Or meet an awful doom from the Lord?

7 Oh, had I angel's wings I would fly, I
would fly,
Oh, had I angel's wings I would fly;
Had I wings like yonder dove,
I soon would soar above,
And see the God I love on his throne.

112.

8s, 8s & 6s. MISS M. BIGLEY.

The Dying Youth.

1 YOUNG men and maids, where'er you be,
Call off your minds from vanity,

And listen what I say:
There was a man, I once did know,
Was living no great while ago,
By death was called away.

2 By sickness, change and fever, bound,
And on his dying bed was found,
And to his father said:
O father, father, you must repent,
And read the holy testament,
And try your soul to save.

3 Before that monster death comes on,
And takes you in his icy arms,
And brings you to your grave.
O father, mother, fare you well—
Your wicked son is going to hell,
To cultivate the flames.

4 Take you my coat of velvet blue,
My pantaloons and waistcoat too—
I give them all to you—
For them I can no longer keep;
A coffin, shroud, and winding sheet,
You must prepare for me.

5 Down, down to hell the sinner goes,
In spite of all his friends or foes,

To cultivate the flames.
Behold him on the rugged wood,
His cross all stained with hallowed blood—
He died for you and I.

113.

P. M.

Mercy is with me wherever I go.

1 TO thee, O my Saviour! to thee will I cling,
For thou art my Lord, my Redeemer and King;
And feeling thy blessing, my spirit shall know
Thy mercy is with me wherever I go.

2 Farewell to the anguish of doubt and despair,
And welcome the rapture of praise and of prayer;
Since meekly confiding in faith, I rejoice
To hear the sweet tones of thy comforting voice.

3 Around me there shineth the heavenly ray,
Which scattereth clouds and their shadows away,

And melteth my soul in devotional glow,
For mercy is with me wherever I go.

4 Farewell to the pleasures which time can afford,
Since thou art my glory, my Saviour and Lord;
Nor fear I the darkness of death and the tomb,
Since thou art my light in the midst of the gloom.

5 Before me there gloweth, around and above,
The pledges of favor, the tokens of love,
And gratitude teacheth my spirit to know,
Thy mercy is with me wherever I go.

114.

C. M.

1 MY soul forsakes her vain delight,
And bids the world farewell;
Base as the dirt beneath my feet,
And mischievous as hell.

2 No longer will I ask your love,
Nor seek your friendship more,
The happiness that I approve,
Is not within your power.

3 There 's nothing round this spacious eart
That suits my large desire;
To boundless joy and solid mirth
My noble thoughts aspire.

4 Had I the pinions of a dove,
I 'd climb the heavenly road;
There sits my Saviour, dressed in love,
And there my smiling God.

115.

P. M.

How lovely the place.

1 HOW lovely the place where the Saviou appears,
To those who believe in his word;
His presence disperses my sorrows anc fears,
And bids me rejoice in my Lord.

2 A day in his courts than a thousand beside,
Is better and lovelier far;
My soul hates the tents where the wicked reside,
And all their delights I abhor.

Lord, give me a place with the humblest of saints,
For low at thy feet I would lie;
I know that thou hearest my feeble complaints,
Thou hearest the young ravens' cry.

Give strength to the souls that now wait upon thee—
O, come in thy chariot of love;
From earth's vain enchantments, O help us to thee,
And set our affections above.

116. *Worthy is the Lamb.*

WORTHY, worthy is the Lamb!
Worthy, worthy is the Lamb!
Worthy, worthy is the Lamb that once was slain!

CHORUS.

Glory, hallelujah!
Praise him, hallelujah!
Glory, hallelujah!
Praise ye the Lord!

Stars of morning, shout for joy,
Sing redemption's mystery!
Holy, holy, holy, cry, praise ye the Lord!
Chorus.

3 Bend thy bow, and whet thy sword!
Send thy Spirit with thy word!
Now revive thy work, O Lord, thou bleed-
ing Lamb! *Chorus.*

4 In this place, and at this hour,
Bare thy arm, display thy power!
Show thyself the conqueror, thou reign-
ing Lamb! *Chorus.*

5 Strike the stoutest sinner through!
Force the cry, "What shall I do?"
Let him weep till born anew, to praise
the Lamb! *Chorus.*

6 Thus we may each moment feel—
Love him, serve him, praise him still,
Till on Zion's holy hill we praise the Lord!
Chorus.

7 And when landed safe above,
In the kingdom of his love, [the Lamb!
We shall all the fullness prove of Christ
Chorus.

8 We the crown of life shall wear,
We the palm of victory bear, [world.
All our Father's glory share in that bright
Chorus.

9 You must all be born anew,
You may all be happy too;
You must all this gate pass through, to
that bright world! *Chorus.*

117.

MRS. L. MAXWELL.

Missionary Hymn.

1 WHEN I first started away from you,
With grief and sorrow, and trouble too,
You gave to me the parting hand,
And wished me safe on the Cumberland.

2 When we were on the ice and snow,
It rained, it hailed—the wind did blow,
And some of us did mourn and cry,
To think with cold we all must die.

3 But bless the Lord, some relief is found,
We 're landed here both safe and sound,
In a lonesome place but fruitful soil,
There 's milk and wine, and corn and oil.

4 I have one more line to write to you—
Religion 's dull, and preachers few;
We 're here in peace, and like to be
With the Indian tribe on the Tennessee.

5 My friends behind, I would like to see,
If from this task I could get free;

To preach I 'm bound, and may it be
With the Indian tribe on the Tennessee.

6 And if on earth we meet no more,
I hope to meet on Canaan's shore;
And there we 'll sing, and happy be,
With the Indian tribe on the Tennessee.

118.

P. M.

The Christian's Comfort.

1 RELIGION, what a glorious treasure,
Filling our hearts with joy and love;
Affording peace and consolation,
It lifts our thoughts to things above.
It calms our fears, it soothes our sorrows,
It smooths our way o'er life's rough sea,
Enkindling patience and holy virtue—
This heavenly portion mine shall be.

2 My flesh and blood shall be dissolved,
And mortal life shall soon be o'er;
All earthly cares and earthly sorrows
Will vex my heart and eyes no more;
But pure religion abides forever, [be,
And my glad heart shall strengthen'd
While endless ages are onward rolling,
This heavenly portion mine shall be.

3 How vain, how fleeting, how transitory,
This world with all its gaudy show;
Its vain delights and deceitful pleasures—
I gladly leave them all below.
But grace and glory shall be my story,
Since I in Jesus such beauties see;
While endless ages are onward rolling,
This heavenly portion mine shall be.

119.

C. P. M. T. GILHAM.

What a Mercy.

1 WHAT a mercy, a mercy is this!
What a mercy, a mercy is this!
What a mercy is this, what a source of joy and bliss!
Jesus died to redeem a lost world.

2 But what will, what will become of me
What will! Oh, what will become of me
What will become of me in life's extremity
If Jesus reigns not in my heart.

3 Despair, sad despair must be my doom!
Despair, sad despair must be my doom!
Yes, despair must be my doom in that world beyond the tomb,
Where his smile can no pleasure impart.

4 But welcome, most welcome, death to me!
But welcome, most welcome, death to me!
Most welcome, death to me, if Christ my portion be,
For his smile shall remove all its smart.

5 Then farewell to sorrow and pain!
Then farewell to sorrow and pain!
Farewell to grief and pain, for dying is my gain,
And the dawn of bright day to my heart.

6 Then, my friends, I must bid you all adieu!
Then, my friends, I must bid you all adieu!
I must bid you all adieu, for my home is full in view,
And my throne, and my crown, and my harp.

7 But we hope—yes, we hope to meet again!
But we hope—yes, we hope to meet again!
We hope to meet again, and with the Saviour reign
In that region of light and of love.

8 Hallelujah to God and the Lamb!
Hallelujah to God and the Lamb!
Hallelujah to the Lamb! Salvation through his name!
Hallelujah to God and the Lamb!

120.

C. M.

The name of Jesus.

1 HOW sweet the name of Jesus sounds
In a believer's ear;
It soothes his sorrows, heals his wounds,
And drives away his fear.

2 It makes the wounded spirit whole,
And calms the troubled breast—
'Tis manna to the hungry soul,
And to the weary, rest.

3 Dear name! the rock on which I build,
My shield and hiding place:
My never-failing treasury filled
With boundless stores of grace.

4 Weak is the effort of my heart,
And cold my warmest thought;
But when I see thee as thou art,
I'll praise thee as I ought.

5 Till then I would thy love proclaim,
With every fleeting breath;
And may the music of thy name
Refresh my soul in death.

121.

P. M.

Christ in the Garden.

1 WHILE nature was sinking in stillness to rest,
The last beam of daylight shone dim in the west,
O'er fields, by pale moonlight, in lonely retreat,
In deep meditation I wandered my feet.

2 While passing a garden, I pausèd to hear
A voice faint and plaintive, from one that was there;
The voice of the sufferer affected my heart,
While pleading in anguish the poor sinner's part.

3 I listened a moment, then turned me to see
What man of compassion this stranger might be;
I saw him low kneeling upon the cold ground,
And felt that his anguish of soul was profound.

4 So deep were his sorrows, so fervent his
prayers,
That down o'er his breast rolled sweat, blood
and tears;
I wept to behold him! I asked him his name!
He answered: 'Tis Jesus—from heaven I
came.

5 I am thy Redeemer: for thee I must die!
The cup is most bitter, but cannot pass by;
Thy sins, like a mountain, are laid upon me,
And all this deep anguish I suffer for thee.

6 How sweet was that moment he made me
rejoice,
His smile, O how pleasant! how cheering
his voice!
I flew from the garden, to spread it abroad:
I shouted salvation, and glory to God.

7 I'm now on my journey to mansions above,
My soul 's full of glory, of light, peace and
love;
I think of the garden, the prayers and the
tears
Of that loving stranger, who banished my
fears.

8 The day of bright glory is rolling around,
When Gabriel descending, the trumpet shall sound,
My soul then in rapture and glory shall rise,
To gaze on the stranger with unclouded eyes.

122.

8s & 6s.
The Revival Hymn

1 THE work of the Lord doth revive,
In grace and in knowledge we thrive;
Our hearts, God is touching—
The day is approaching—
Sing glory, hallelujah! Amen.

2 Lo! heralds are flying abroad,
To point out the heavenly road;
The bright sun is beaming,
Rich mercy is streaming—
Sing glory, hallelujah! Amen.

3 The Saviour and friend of mankind,
Gives comfort and peace to the mind;
The weary he blesses—
Removes their distresses:
Sing glory, hallelujah! Amen.

4 Rich fruit in abundance doth grow,
The earth shall with glory o'erflow!

Jehovah hath spoken,
His word can't be broken!
Give him glory, hallelujah! Amen.

5 Pure streams in the desert shall spring,
The hills and the valleys shall ring,
While cherubs adore him,
And fall down before him:
Sing glory, hallelujah! Amen.

6 O'er angels and men he doth reign!
His right he shall ever maintain;
His foes he 's o'erthrowing—
His empire is growing:
Hallelujah! hallelujah! Amen.

123.

P. M.

Poor Sinner, Think.

1 O YE young, ye gay, ye proud,
You must die and wear the shroud;
Time will rob you of your bloom—
Death will drag you to the tomb.

CHORUS.

Then you 'll cry: I want to be
Happy in eternity.

2 Will you go to heaven or hell?
One you must, and there to dwell;

Christ will come, and quickly too :
I must meet him : so must you.
Chorus.

3 The judgment throne will soon appear—
All the world must then draw near;
Sinners will be driven down,
Saints will wear a starry crown.
Chorus.

124.

P. M.

The Christian's Song.

1 JOYFULLY, joyfully, onward I move,
Bound for the land of bright spirits above;
Angelic choristers sing as I come:
Joyfully, joyfully, haste to thy home.

2 Soon, with my pilgrimage ended below
Home to that land of delight will I go;
Pilgrim and stranger no more shall I roam,
Joyfully, joyfully, resting at home.

3 Friends who have loved me have passed on before,
Waiting, they watch me approaching the shore,
Singing, to cheer me through death's chilling gloom—
Joyfully, joyfully, haste to thy home.

4 Death, with thy weapons of war lay me
low,
Strike, king of terrors, I fear not the blow;
Jesus hath broken the bars of the tomb—
Joyfully, joyfully, will I go home.

5 Bright will the morn of eternity dawn—
Death shall be banished—his sceptre be
gone;
Joyfully then shall I witness his doom—
Joyfully, joyfully, safely at home.

125.

P. M. MRS. M. CARPENTER.

A Mother's Consolation.

1 FAREWELL, lov'd ones; death hath
torn you
From a mother's fond embrace;
I am left alone in sorrow,
Never more to see your face.

2 From this world of pain and anguish,
You have fled for joys above;
All your sorrows now are ended,
You are bless'd with Jesus' love.

3 In that blissful world I'll meet you,
When the storms of life are past—

There to range the groves of pleasure,
While eternal ages last.

4 Hark! I hear a voice from heaven,
Bids me banish all my fears;
Those you grieve are only sleeping—
Weeping mother, dry thy tears.

5 Sleep on, lov'd ones! none disturb you,
Sleep till Jesus bids you rise!
Then, with all God's ransomed people,
I will meet you in the skies.

126.

P. M. A. NISWANGER.

We love Friendship.

1 THE reason we love friendship
We will deny to no man;
How shall, how shall, how shall we,
Who are thus formed for happiness,
E'er slight a loving Christian?
Since Jesus, Jesus hath died on the tree,
For to deliver man
From violence and treason—
That we might love each other,
And seek our soul's salvation.
'Twas love that moved the mighty God,
For to redeem the nations,
That happy, happy they might be.

2 On the feast day in ancient times,
Jesus stood thus crying:
Whoso thirsteth, let every man
Come unto me and freely drink,
And thus be saved from dying;
For surely, surely, nothing else can
Quench the immortal thirst
That in your heart is glowing. [grace
Come, then, and drink the streams of
Which are so freely flowing,
Saying, drink, my love, my only dove,
For you it is a flowing—
Then happy, happy you shall be.

3 Let us, who have begun to taste
The sweets of this salvation,
Follow, follow—let us follow on,
Believing we shall overcome,
Resisting all temptation.
Since Jesus, Jesus—since Jesus, the Son,
With outstretched arms,
And voice that 's so inviting
To purling streams of purest joys
Is thus our souls exciting,
Let us impart to him our hearts,
By faith and love uniting—
Then happy, happy we shall be.

127.

P. M.

A call to the Young.

1 YOUNG people who delight in sin,
I'll tell you what has lately been:
A lady who was young and fair,
Who died in sin and sad despair.

2 She'd go to frolics, dance and play,
In spite of all her friends could say;
"I'll turn to God when I get old,
And he will then receive my soul."

3 On Friday morning she took sick,
Her stubborn heart began to break —
Alas! alas! my days are spent;
Too late, too late, for to repent.

4 She called her mother to her bed
And thus in dying anguish said:
When I am dead, remember well,
Your only daughter screams in hell!

5 She gnawed her tongue before she died—
She roll'd and groan'd, she scream'd and cried:
Oh! must I burn forevermore,
Till thousand, thousand years are o'er?

6 Young people, lest this be your case,
Return to God and seek his face;
Upon your knees for mercy cry,
Lest you in sin like Mary die.

128.

P. M.

Resurrection.

1 MARY to the Saviour's tomb,
Hasted at the early dawn;
Spice she brought, and rich perfume,
But the Lord she lov'd had gone.
For a while she lingering stood,
Fill'd with sorrow and surprise —
Trembling while a crystal flood
Issued from her weeping eyes.

2 But her sorrows quickly fled,
When she heard his welcome voice;
Christ has risen from the dead—
Now he bids her heart rejoice.
What a change his word can make,
Turning darkness into day;
Ye who weep for Jesus' sake,
He will wipe your tears away

3 He who came to comfort her
When she thought her all was lost,

Will for your relief appear,
  Though you now are tempest tost.
On his arm your burden cast—
  On his love your thoughts employ;
Weeping for a while may last,
  But the morning brings the joy.

129.

L. M. DAVID DESELMS.

None but Jesus.

1 JESUS, my all, to heaven is gone,
He whom I fix my hopes upon;
His track I see, and I'll pursue
The narrow way till him I view.

2 The way the holy prophets went—
The road that leads from banishment—
The king's highway of holiness
I'll go, for all his paths are peace.

3 This is the way I long have sought,
And mourn'd because I found it not;
My grief and burden long has been,
Because I could not cease from sin.

4 The more I strove against its power,
I felt its weight and guilt the more,
Till late I heard my Saviour say:
Come hither, soul, I am the way.

5 Lo, glad I come, and thou, blest Lamb,
Shall take me to thee as I am;
Nothing but sin have I to give—
Nothing but love shall I receive.

6 Then will I tell to sinners round,
What a dear Saviour I have found—
I'll point to thy redeeming blood,
And say, Behold the way to God!

130. *Death.* C. M.

1 WHEN those we love are snatch'd away
By death's resistless hand,
Our hearts the mournful tribute pay,
Which pity must demand.

2 While pity prompts the rising sigh,
O may this truth, impressed
With awful power, "I too must die,"
Sink deep in every breast.

3 Let this vain world engage no more—
Behold the gaping tomb,
It bids us seize the present hour,
To-morrow death may come.

4 The voice of this alarming scene
May every heart obey—

Nor be the heavenly warning vain,
Which calls to watch and pray.

5 O, let us fly—to Jesus fly,
Whose powerful arm can save,
Then shall our hopes ascend on high,
And triumph o'er the grave.

6 Great God! thy sovereign grace impart,
With cleansing, healing power;
This only can prepare the heart
For death's surprising hour.

131.

8s.

The Christian's Hope.

1 MY gracious Redeemer I love,
His praises aloud I'll proclaim,
And join with the armies above,
To shout his adorable name:
To gaze on his glories divine,
Shall be my eternal employ—
And feel them incessantly shine,
My boundless, ineffable joy.

2 He freely redeemed with his blood,
My soul from the confines of hell,
To live on the smiles of my God,
And in his sweet presence to dwell.

To shine with the angels of light—
With saints and with seraphs to sing,
To view with eternal delight,
My Jesus, my Saviour, my King.

3 In Meshec, as yet, I reside,
A darksome and restless abode;
Molested with foes on each side,
And longing to dwell with my God.
O, when shall my spirit exchange
This cell of corruptible clay,
For mansions celestial, and range
Through realms of ineffable day?

4 My glorious Redeemer! I long
To see thee descend on the cloud,
Amidst the bright, numberless throng,
And mix with the triumphing crowd.
Oh, when wilt thou bid me ascend,
To join in thy praises above;
To gaze on the world without end,
And feast on thy ravishing love?

5 Nor sorrow, nor sickness, nor pain,
Nor sin, nor temptation, nor fear,
Shall ever molest me again—
Perfection of glory reigns there.

This soul and this body shall shine
  In robes of salvation and praise,
And banquet on pleasures divine,
  Where God his full beauty displays.

6 Ye palaces, sceptres, and crowns,
  Your pride with disdain I survey;
Your pomps are but shadows and sounds,
  And pass in a moment away.
The crown that my Saviour bestows,
  Yon permanent sun shall outshine;
My joy everlastingly flows—
  My God, my Redeemer, is mine.

132.

7s & 6s.

1 O, WHEN shall I see Jesus,
  And reign with him above,
And from the flowing fountain
  Drink everlasting love?
When shall I be delivered
  From this vain world of sin,
And with my blessed Jesus,
  Drink endless pleasures in?

2 But now I am a soldier,
  My Captain 's gone before;
He 's given me my orders,
  And bid me not give o'er.

His promises are faithful—
  A righteous crown he 'll give,
And all his valiant soldiers
  Eternally shall live.

3 Through grace, I am determined
  To conquer, though I die;
And then away to Jesus,
  On wings of love I 'll fly.
Farewell to sin and sorrow,
  I bid you both adieu;
And O, my friends, prove faithful,
  And on your way pursue.

4 Whene'er you meet with troubles
  And trials on your way,
Then cast your care on Jesus,
  And do n't forget to pray.
Gird on the heavenly armor
  Of faith, and hope, and love;
And when the combat 's ended,
  He 'll carry you above.

5 O do not be discouraged,
  For Jesus is your friend,
And if you want more knowledge,
  He 'll not refuse to lend;

Neither will he upbraid you,
Though oftener you request—
He 'll give you grace to conquer,
And take you home to rest.

133.

P. M. 8s & 7s.

Christ, the Lamb.

1 HARK! ten thousand harps and voices
Sound the note of praise above—
Jesus reigns, and heaven rejoices,
Jesus reigns, the God of love;
See! he sits on yonder throne—
Jesus rules the world alone.

CHORUS.

Hallelujah! Hallelujah!
Hallelujah! Amen.

2 Jesus, hail! whose glory brightens
All above, and gives it worth—
Lord of life! thy smile enlightens,
Cheers and charms thy saints on earth;
When we think of love like thine—
Lord, we own it love divine.
Chorus.

3 King of glory, reign forever!
Thine an everlasting crown;

Nothing from thy love shall sever
  Those whom thou hast made thine own—
Happy objects of thy grace,
Destined to behold thy face.
Chorus.

4 Saviour, hasten thine appearing!
  Bring, O, bring the glorious day,
When the awful summons hearing,
  Heaven and earth shall pass away;
Then, with golden harps, we 'll sing
Glory, glory to our King!—*Chorus.*

134.

C. M.

1 All hail the power of Jesus' name—
  Let angels prostrate fall;
Bring forth the royal diadem,
  And crown him Lord of all.

2 Crown him, ye martyrs of our God,
  Who from his altar call;
Extol the stem of Jesse's rod,
  And crown him Lord of all.

3 Ye chosen seed of Israel's race,
  A remnant weak and small,
Hail him who saves you by his grace,
  And crown him Lord of all.

4 Ye Gentile sinners, ne'er forget
The wormwood and the gall;
Go spread your trophies at his feet,
And crown him Lord of all.

5 Let every kindred, every tribe
On this terrestrial ball,
To him all majesty ascribe,
And crown him Lord of all.

6 O, that with yonder sacred throng,
We at his feet may fall;
We 'll join the everlasting song,
And crown him Lord of all.

135.

S. M.

1 COME, we that love the Lord,
And let our joys be known;
Join in a song with sweet accord,
And thus surround the throne.

2 The sorrows of the mind,
Be banish'd from the place;
Religion never was design'd
To make our pleasures less.

3 Let those refuse to sing,
That never knew our God;

But children of the heavenly King
May speak their joys abroad.

4 The men of grace have found
Glory begun below;
Celestial fruits, on earthly ground,
From faith and hope may grow.

5 The hill of Zion yields
A thousand sacred sweets,
Before we reach the heavenly fields,
Or walk the golden streets.

6 Then let our songs abound,
And every tear be dry; [ground,
We 're marching through Immanuel's
To fairer worlds on high.

136.

P. M. Rev. T. Jones.

The Beautiful Valley.

1 'T IS low down in that beautiful valley,
Where love crowns the meek and the lowly—
Where no storms of envy or folly
Can ever roll their billows again.
The meek soul, in humble subjection,
Can there find unshaken protection—
There soft gales of cheering reflection—
The mind soothed from sorrow and pain.

2 This low vale is far from contention,
Where no soul can dream of dissension—
Where no wiles of evil intention
Can find out these regions of peace.
'T is there, there, the Lord will deliver,
And souls drink of that beautiful river,
Where flows peace forever and ever,
And love and joy forever increase.

3 'T is there, those who, by storms have been driven,
Shall moor their barks in that beautiful haven;
And there bask in the sunshine of heaven,
And triumph in Immanuel's name.
'T is there, there, in yonder bright glory,
We 'll shout, and sing, and tell the glad story;
When we have passed old Jordan quite over,
We 'll sing hallelujah to God and the Lamb.

137.

ASA NISWANGER.

The Christian Warfare.

1 HARK, brethren! don't you hear the sound?
The martial trumpets are now blowing,

Men in orders listing round,
  And soldiers to the standard flowing;
Bounty offered—joy and peace—
  To every soldier this is given,
When from toils of war they cease:
  A mansion bright prepared in heaven.

2 Those who long in sin have lain,
  And felt the hand of dire oppression,
Are now relieved from Satan's chain,
  And they endowed with large possession.
The poor, the sick, the blind, the lame—
  Their maladies are also healed;
Outlawed rebels, when they come,
  Receive a pardon freely sealed.

3 The battle is not to the strong!
  The burden's on our Captain's shoulder;
None so aged or so young,
  But may enlist and be a soldier.
Those who cannot fight or fly,
  Beneath his banner find protection;
None who on his name rely,
  Shall be reduced to base subjection.

4 You need not fear—the cause is good!
  Come, who will to the crown aspire?

In this cause the martyrs bled,
Or shouted victory in the fire.
In this cause let 's follow on,
And soon we 'll tell the pleasing story,
How, by faith, we gained the crown,
And fought our way to life and glory.

5 The battle, brethren, is begun!
Behold the army now in motion!
Some, by faith, behold the crown,
And almost grasp their future portion.
Hark! the victor 's singing loud, [ling!
Immanuel's chariot wheels are rumb-
Mourners weeping through the crowd,
And Satan's kingdom down is tumbling.

6 Hark, ye rebels! come and list,
The officers are now recruiting;
Why will you in sin persist,
Or spend your time in vain disputing?
All your cavils sure are vain,
For if you do not sue for favor,
Down you 'll sink to endless pain,
To bear the wrath of God forever.

138.

L. M. D. ASA NISWANGER.

Time.

1 TIME speeds away, away, away—
Another hour—another day;
Another month—another year
Drop from us like the leaflets sear;
Drop like the life-blood from our hearts—
The rosebloom from the cheek departs,
The tresses from the temples fall,
The eyes grow dim and strange to all.

2 Time speeds away, away, away,
Like torrent in a stormy day;
He undermines the stately tower,
Uproots the tree and snaps the flower,
And sweeps from our distracted breast,
The friends that loved—the friends that blessed,
And leaves us weeping on the shore,
To which they can return no more.

3 Time speeds away, away, away—
No eagle through the skies of day,
No wind along the hills can flee
So swiftly or so smooth as he.
Like fiery steed—from stage to stage,
He bears us on—from youth to age,

Then plunges in the fearful sea
Of fathomless eternity.

139.

P. M. Asa Niswanger.

The Poor Backslider.

1 WHEN I call to my remembrance
My former happy days!
My days were spent in pleasure,
My nights in prayer and praise.
But since I 've lost my Saviour,
My prayer has been in vain;
"Yet come, backsliding sinner,
You still may come again."

2 I have fled away, like Jonah,
The presence of my God;
Like Peter, I denied him,
And trampled on his blood;
Like Judas, I have sold him,
For pelf and earthly gain—
"Yet come, backsliding sinner,
You still may come again."

3 I have sinned against the light—
Too long against his grace;
I've grieved his Holy Spirit,
And mocked him to his face.

My sins they cry for vengeance,
Like those of wretched Cain;
"Yet come, backsliding sinner,
You still may come again."

4 Reflecting now, with sorrow,
On pleasures long since dead,
I felt an inward heaven,
But now a constant hell.
I am sinking, I am dying,
I feel increasing pain—
"Yet come, backsliding sinner,
You still may come again."

5 Hark! is not that my Saviour's voice?
It speaks along the skies,
It bids my mourning soul rejoice,
It bids me now arise—
"Arise! come to thy Saviour!
I'll not thy tears disdain—
Yes, poor backsliding sinner,
You still may come again.

6 "I'll clasp thee to my bosom,
And wash thee in my blood;
Heal all thy past backslidings,
And fill thee with my love.

My oath is pledged, and promise,
That none shall come in vain;
So, poor backsliding sinner,
Thy soul shall live again."

140.

C. M. ASA NISWANGER.

Something New.

1 SINCE man, by sin, has lost his God,
He seeks creation through,
And vainly hopes for solid bliss,
In trying something new.

2 The new possess'd, like fading flowers,
Soon loses its gay hue;
The bubble now no longer takes—
The soul wants something new.

3 And could we call all Europe ours,
With India and Peru,
The mind would feel an aching void,
And still want something new.

4 But when we feel a Saviour's love,
All good in him we view;
The soul forsakes its vain delights—
In Christ finds something new.

5 The joys the dear Redeemer brings
Will bear a strict review;

Nor need we ever change again
  For Christ is always new.

141.

P. M. Asa Niswanger.

1 O, THAT I had some humble place,
  Where I might hide from sorrow—
Where I might see my Saviour's face,
  And there be freed from terror.
O had I wings like Noah's dove,
  I'd leave this world and Satan,
And fly away to realms above,
  Where Jesus stands inviting.

2 My heart is often made to mourn,
  Because I'm faint and feeble—
And when my Saviour seems to frown
  My soul is filled with trouble;
But when he doth again return,
  And I repent my folly,
'Tis then I after glory run,
  And still my Jesus follow.

3 I have my bitter and my sweet,
  While through this world I travel;
Sometimes I shout and often weep,
  Which makes my foes to marvel.
But let them think, and think again,
  I feel I'm bound for heaven—

I hope I shall with Jesus reign,
I therefore still will praise him.

4 I want to live a Christian here —
I want to die while shouting;
I want to feel my Saviour near,
When soul and body's parting.
I want to see bright angels stand,
And waiting to receive me—
To bear my soul to Canaan's land,
Where Christ is gone before me.

142.

P. M. ASA NISWANGER.

1 WHEN I set out for glory,
I left the world behind,
Determined for a city
That's out of sight to find.

CHORUS.

And to glory I will go,
And to glory I will go, I'll go, I'll go,
And to glory I will go.

2 I left my worldly honor—
I left my worldly fame—
I left my young companions,
And with them, my good name.

3 Some said I'd better tarry,
They thought I was too young
For to prepare for dying,
But that was all my theme.

4 Come all my loving brethren
And listen to my cry:
All you that are backsliders
Must shortly beg or die.

CHORUS.

And to begging I will go,
And to begging I will go, will go, will go,
And to begging I will go.

5 The Lord he loves the beggar,
Who truly begs indeed;
He always will relieve him
Whene'er he stands in need.

6 I do not beg for riches,
Nor to be dressed fine—
The garment that he'll give me,
The sun it will outshine.

7 I'm not asham'd to beg
While here on earth I stay—
I'm not ashamed to watch,
I'm not ashamed to pray.

8 The richest man I ever saw
Was one that begged the most,
His soul was filled with Jesus,
And with the Holy Ghost.

9 And now we are encouraged,
Come let us travel on,
Until we join the angels
And sing the holy song.
And to glory I will go, &c.

143. P. M. Asa Niswanger.

1 COME sisters and brothers, who love one another,
And have done so for years that are gone,
How often we've met him in sweet heavenly union,
Who opens the way to God's throne!
With joy and thanksgiving, we 'll praise him who loved us,
While we run in the bright shining way;
Though we part here in body, we 're bound for one glory,
And bound for each other to pray.

2 There was Joshua and Joseph, Elias and Moses,
Who prayed as they journeyed along;

There was Abra'm and Isaac, and Jacob and David,
And Solomon, Stephen and John.
There was Simeon and Anna, and I do'nt know how many,
Who prayed, and God heard from his throne;
Some cast among lions, some bound with rough irons,
Yet glory and praises they sung.

3 Some tell us that praying, and also that praising,
Is labor that 's all spent in vain;
But we have such witness that God hears with swiftness,
From praying we will not refrain.
There was old father Noah, and ten thousand more,
Who witnessed that God heard them pray;
There was Samuel and Hannah, Paul, Silas and Peter
And Daniel and Jonah we 'll say.

4 That God, by his spirit, or an angel, doth visit
Our souls and our bodies while praying;

Shall we all go fainting, while they all go praising,
And glorify God in the flame?
God grant us to inherit the same praying spirit,
While onward we journey below;
So that when we cease praying we may not cease praising,
But around God's bright throne we may bow.

144.

8s & 7s. Asa Niswanger.

Autumn.

1 HAIL! ye sighing sons of sorrow!
Learn with me your certain doom;
Learn with me your fate to-morrow—
Dead—perhaps laid in the tomb.
See all nature fading, dying,
Silent, all things seem to mourn;
Life, from vegetation flying,
Calls to mind the mouldering urn.

2 Lo, in yonder forest standing,
Lofty cedars—how they nod;
Scenes of nature—how surprising,
Read in nature nature's God.
While the annual frosts are cropping
Leaves and tendrils from the trees,

So our friends are yearly dropping;
We are like to one of these.

3 Hollow winds about me roaring,
Noisy waters round me rise—
While I sit, my fate deploring,
Tears fast streaming from my eyes.
What to me is autumn's treasure,
Since I know no earthly joy;
Long I've lost all youthful pleasure—
Time will health and youth destroy.

4 Former friends—how oft I ve sought them,
Just to cheer a troubled mind;
Now they 're gone, like leaves of autumn,
Driv'n before the dreary wind.
When a few more days are wasted,
And a few more scenes are o'er—
When a few more griefs I 've tasted,
I shall rise to fall no more.

5 Fast my sun of life 's declining—
Soon 't will set in endless night;
But my hopes, pure and reviving,
Rise to fairer worlds of light.
Cease this trembling, mourning, sighing,
Death shall burst this sullen gloom;

Then, my spirit, fluttering, flying,
Shall be borne beyond the tomb.

145.

P. M. Asa Niswanger.

1 HARK! my soul, it is the Lord!
'Tis thy Saviour—hear his word!
Jesus speaks, and speaks to thee—
Say, poor sinner, "lov'st thou me?"

2 I delivered thee when bound,
And when wounded healed thy wound—
Sought thee wandering—set thee right—
Turned thy darkness into light.

3 "Can a woman's tender cares
Cease towards the child she bears?
Yes, she may forgetful be,
Yet I will remember thee.

4 "Mine is an unchanging love,
Higher than the heights above;
Deeper than the depths beneath—
Free and faithful—strong as death!

5 "Thou shalt see my glory soon,
When the work of grace is done;
Partners of my throne shall be:
Say, poor sinner, lov'st thou me?"

6 Lord, it is my chief complaint,
That my love is weak and faint;
Yet I love thee, and adore—
O for grace to love thee more.

146.

C. M. ASA NISWANGER.

Victory over Death.

1 LORD, at thy temple we appear,
As happy Simeon came,
And hope to meet our Saviour here:
O make our joys the same.

2 With what divine and vast delight,
The good old man was filled,
When fondly in his withered arms,
He clasped the holy child.

3 "Now I can leave this world, he cried,
Behold thy servant dies!
I 've seen thy great salvation, Lord,
And close my peaceful eyes.

4 "This is the light prepared to shine
Upon the Gentile lands;
Thine Israel's glory, and their hope,
To break their slavish bands."

5 Jesus, the vision of thy face
Hath overpowering charms;
Scarce shall I feel death's cold embrace,
If Christ be in my arms.

6 Then while ye hear my heart-strings break,
How sweet my moments roll;
A mortal paleness on my cheek,
And glory in my soul.

147.

A. L. Marrison.

The Thief on the Cross.

1 AS on the cross the Saviour hung,
He groaned, and bled and died;
He poured salvation on a wretch
Who languished by his side.
His crimes, with inward guilt and shame,
The penitent confessed,
Then turned his dying eyes to Christ,
And thus his prayer addressed:

2 Jesus, thou Son and heir of heaven!
Thou spotless Lamb of God!
I see thee bathed in sweat and tears,
And weltering in thy blood;
But quickly from these scenes of woe,
In triumph thou shalt rise—

Burst through the gloom and shades of death,
And reign above the skies.

3 Amidst the glory of that world,
Dear Saviour, think on me,
And in the victory of thy blood
Let me a sharer be.
His prayer the dying Jesus heard,
And instantly replies:
To-day thy parting soul shall be
With me in Paradise.

4 Oh then, poor mourner, do n't despair,
He ever lives the same,
Presenting at the Father's throne,
That you may know his name.
Believe his word, and you shall know
Your sins are all forgiven;
Live happy here, and die in peace,
And rise and shine in heaven.

148.

MISS M. A. WEST.

1 MY friends and my neighbors, who live in this place,
Come listen awhile, and I 'll tell you your case:

You have slighted the gospel, despised God's word,
And scoffed at the preachers that were sent by the Lord.

2 There's many a good sermon you've heard in this place,
To warn you of sinning, and teach you God's grace;
But now may the preachers complain to the Lord,
And mourn that the people have rejected his word.

3 Some, under affliction, will appear for to mourn,
And when in sharp sickness, they promise to return;
But if the Lord spares them, they will return to their sin,
To drinking and swearing, and to dancing again.

4 Sinners, you are left in a dangerous case,
You can rail at God's people—and that in their face;

You make yourselves merry, but friends you do n't know—
God's vengeance pursues you wherever you go.

5 We read that the wicked shall be turned into hell,
And all that forget God, with devils must dwell;
I pray you be entreated to turn to the Lord:
Whilst mercy is offered, be led by his word.

6 Farewell, my dear friends! I must bid you farewell!
The love that I have for you, there 's no tongue can tell;
And I wish, above all things, we all may prepare
To meet Christ in glory, and reign with him there.

149.

MISS S. PILCHER.

1 PALE, motionless and silent, lay
An infant on its bed,
While on its face a smile of peace—
A beauteous halo shed;
And on that face a mother gazed,
With looks of wild despair,

Conscious that death's resistless hand
Had fixed his signet there.

2 She saw alone the hastening hour
When to her fond caress,
No more she might those ruby lips
With tenderest rapture press;
But saw not in that placid smile
The brighter vision sealed,
Which on her darling's spirit broke—
To her yet unrevealed.

3 For near the couch an angel spread
His pure ethereal wings,
Imparting to that spotless soul
Unutterable things;
And whispered soft of anguish spared—
Of bliss immortal given;
And all its new-born senses filled
With dreams of opening heaven.

150.

ALEXANDER T. ORR.

1 A STORY most lovely I 'll tell,
Concerning the Lord from the skies;
He suffered, it is known very well,
That sinners, poor sinners, might rise.

He left his exalted abode,
  For man by trangression was lost;
He appeased the wrath of our God,
  Consenting to die on the cross.

2 O, was it for crimes I have done,
  My Saviour was hailed with a kiss
By Judas, the traitorous man?
  Was ever such mercy as this?
The rebels, all joined in a band,
  Confined him and led him away;
The cords were wrapped round his soft hands—
  O look at him, sinners, I pray.

3 At Pilate's stone pillar he lay—
  His body was scourged with a whip;
Not one of them ever did hear
  A railing word fall from his lips.
They made him a crown out of thorns—
  Our Jesus they did so abuse; [scorn,
They mock'd him, and laughed him to
  And hailed him the King of the Jews.

4 They ladened the Lamb with the cross,
  They drove him up Calvary's hill;
Stop, mourners, a moment, and pause—
  All nature was silent and still.

They rushed the nails through his hands,
The blood also flowed from his feet—
Behold him—how passive he stands;
To look at the sight—it was great.

5 He cries: Oh my Father and God!
You've left me to suffer in pain;
The cross was all covered with blood,
The temple's vail rented in twain.
He groaned his last when he died,
The sun he refused to shine;
They rushed the spear in his side—
This loving Redeemer was mine.

6 He fought the hard battle, and won
His kingdom, and offered it free;
Oh, Christians, look forward and run—
That kingdom I hope we shall see.
I long to mount up to the skies—
In paradise make my abode;
To sing with bright angels on high,
And rest with my pacified God.

150. *Come, Come Away.*

1 OH, come, come away, from labor now reposing;
Oh come, come away;
Let anxious care awhile forbear,

Oh come, our sacred joys renew,
And there where faith will strengthen you,
And Christ will welcome you,
Oh come, come away.

2 From toil and the cares on which the day is closing,
The hour of eve brings sweet reprieve,
Oh come, come away;
Oh come where God will smile on thee,
And in our hearts will rapture be,
And time pass happily,
Oh come, come away.

3 While tun'd to God's love, the angels' harps are ringing,
And sound his praise through endless days,
Oh come, come away;
In answering songs of sympathy,
We 'll sing in tuneful harmony,
From earth's temptations free,
Oh come, come away.

4 The bright day is gone, the moon and stars appearing,
With silver light illume the night,
Oh come, come away;

Come join your prayers with ours—
address
Kind heaven, our meeting here to bless
With peace, hope, happiness,
Oh come, come away.

152.

The Harp. A. J. CAVANAUGH.

1 COME, brothers and sisters, and hear me relate,
And I will inform you of my present state:
Though often I have called sweet Jesus my own,
I often feel rejected—like one left alone.

2 How backward in duty, how lifeless I be,
The smiles of my Saviour how seldom I see!
I scarcely in Zion can raise a sweet song—
My harp on the willow now seems to be hung.

3 I know prayer 's a duty I owe to the Lord,
Enjoined there upon me in his holy word;
But when I attempt it I have no heart to pray,
My thoughts are so wavering, and often astray.

4 But when I read the Scripture, instruction to gain,
'Tis but a small portion that I can retain;
They seem so mysterious and dark to my view,
I can 't understand them, as I 'd wish to do.

5 In all my performances how short do I fall—
I am pining and languishing, and barren withal;
I seem as a tree that encumbers the ground,
The leaves make appearance, but no fruit is found.

6 My moments are lonesome—small comforts I find,
Dark clouds hover o'er me, and darken my mind;
The cold dreary winter with tempest doth blow—
I am chilled with the cold, and in darkness I go.

7 Disperse these dark clouds, O dear Jesus, my friend,
And cause this cold winter in summer to end;

Thy soul-cheering presence to me now restore,
And give me my harp from the willow once more.

153.

JAMES A. CAVANAUGH.

A new and noble Song.

1 SING to the Lord, ye distant lands,
Ye tribes of every tongue;
His new discovered grace demands
A new and noble song.

2 Say to the nations Jesus reigns,
God's own Almighty Son;
His power the sinking world sustains,
And grace surrounds his throne.

3 Let heaven proclaim the joyful day—
Joy through the earth be seen;
Let cities shine in bright array,
And fields in cheerful green.

4 The joyous earth, the bending skies,
His glorious truth display;
Ye mountains sink—ye valleys rise!
Prepare the Lord his way.

5 Behold he comes! he comes to bless
The nations as their God;

To show the world his righteousness,
And send his truth abroad.

154.

Missionary Hymn.

PART I.

1 I CAME to the spot where the white pilgrim lay,
And pensively stood by his tomb,
When in a low whisper I heard something say,
"How sweetly I sleep here alone!

2 "The tempest may howl, and the loud thunders roll,
The gathering storms may arise;
Yet calm are my feelings, at rest is my soul,
The tears are all wiped from these eyes.

3 "The cause of my Master compelled me from home;
I bade my companions farewell;
I left my sweet children, who now for me mourn,
In far distant regions to dwell.

4 "I wandered, an exile and stranger below,
To publish salvation abroad;

The trump of the gospel endeavor to blow,
Inviting poor sinners to God.

5 "But, when among strangers and far from my home,
No kindred or relative nigh,
I met the contagion and sank in the tomb—
My spirit to mansions on high.

6 "Oh, tell my companions and children most dear,
To weep not for Joseph, though gone;
The same hand that led me through scenes dark and drear
Has kindly assisted me home."

PART II.

1 I called at the house of the mourner below—
I entered the mansion of grief,
The tears of deep sorrow most freely did flow—
I tried, but could give no relief.

2 There sat a lone widow, dejected and sad,
By affliction and sorrow oppressed;
And there were her children, in mourning arrayed,
And sighs were escaping each breast.

3 I spoke to the widow concerning her grief,
I asked for the cause of her woe,
And why there was nothing could give her relief,
Or soothe her deep sorrow below!

4 She looked at the children, then looked upon me;
That look I shall never forget;
More eloquent far than a seraph can be—
It spoke of the troubles she met

5 "The hand of affliction falls heavily now;
I am left with my children to mourn,
The friend of my youth lies silent and low,
In yonder cold graveyard alone.

6 "But why should I mourn, or feel to complain,
Or think that my fortune is hard?
Have I met with affliction?—'tis truly his gain—
He entered the joy of his Lord.

7 "His work is completed and finished below;
His last tear has fallen, I trust;

He has preached his last sermon, and met his last foe—
Has conquered, and is now at rest!"

155. *To the memory of Maria Roush, who died March 1st,* 1813—*Boon county, Ky.*

PART I.

1 YOUNG ladies all, attention give,
You that in wicked pleasure-live;
One of your sex, the other day,
Was snatched, by death's cold hand, away.

2 This lesson she has left for you—
To teach the careless what to do,
To seek Jehovah while they live,
And everlasting honors give.

3 Awhile before this damsel died,
Her tongue was speechless, bound and tied;
At length she opened wide her eyes,
And said her tongue was liberized.

4 She called her father to her bed,
And thus in dying anguish said:
My days on earth are at an end,
My soul is summoned to attend

5 Before Jehovah's burning bar,
To hear my awful sentence there;
From meetings you have kept your child,
To pleasures wanton, vain and wild,

6 To frolics you would let me go,
And dance my soul to pain and woe;
But now, dear father, do repent,
And read the holy testament.

7 Your head is blossomed for the grave—
You have a precious soul to save;
Your children teach to serve the Lord,
And worship him with one accord.

PART II.

1 Her honored mother she addressed,
Whose tears were streaming down her breast;
She grasped her tender hand and said:
Remember me when I am dead.

2 Your aged years have rolled away,
And brought you to the present day;
Now take your dying child's advice,
And turn from sin and avarice,

3 Before the golden bowl be broke,
Or life's fair chord receive a stroke;

Before death's banner round you wave,
Before you 're summoned to the grave.

4 I see no pleasure here on earth,
To trace from death back to my birth,
That would entice my soul to stay
In this vain world of misery.

5 By faith I view the distant shore,
Where pleasures reign forevermore,
Where songs on seraphs' pinions rise,
Beyond the curtain of the skies.

6 Prepare yourself, oh mother dear,
For you are now on the frontier,
Where everlasting time shall roll
Around my poor departing soul.

7 Her weeping brother she addressed,
And thus her faltering tongue expressed:
Forsake your sins, and turn to God,
And fear the vengeance of his rod.

8 Or he will send you down to hell,
Forever in the lake to dwell,
Where fiery billows bursting roll
Around the never-dying soul.

9 Life is the time to seek his face,
His gospel, mercy, and his grace;
His arms are now extended wide—
Come purchase peace, the prophet cried.

PART III.

1 Now give yourself up to his trust,
Before your body turns to dust;
And while you breathe the vital air,
Pour out your precious soul in prayer;

2 Reform your life in word and deed,
And pray that Christ may intercede
For you and for my sister dear,
Who now is weeping by me here.

3 O, sister, come and take your leave—
Don't break your heart, O do not grieve;
Chill'd are my limbs, the damps of death
Run down my cheeks and steal my breath.

4 See, o'er my head, how angels shine
In sparkling garments, long and fine,
To soothe my parting spirit here,
And wipe away the briny tear.

5 Now my immortal soul shall rise
To God's eternal paradise,

Where crowds of angels round him stand,
And cherubs fly at his command.

6 My body here must slumbering lie,
'Till Gabriel's trump shall rend the sky;
Then in the resurrection day,
When heaven and earth shall pass away,

7 I hope you 'll meet me far above,
Where all is harmony and love;
Once more, dear kindred, let me tell,
I bid you all a long farewell.

8 At this she closed her eyes in death,
And thus resigned her mortal breath;
Under death's solemn cypress shade,
They placed this young departed maid.

9 While friends and kindred went around,
To see her corpse laid in the ground,
A warning to the human race,
For all must go into that place.

10 To the cold grave where silence reigns,
In death's tremendous dark domains;
Young people all, a warning take,
And from your wicked pleasures break.

156.

8s. P. M. ASA NISWANGER.

1 THUS saith the Lord of glory:
I'd have the world to know me,
As they must stand before me,
To account for all they have done.
I am the God of heaven—
Eternally I am living;
All things are my creation,
For I am God alone.

2 Oh, will you be converted,
And to my ways conformed—
A ransom is provided,
If you will only come;
But if you do refuse it,
I never will excuse it,
Because you do refuse it,
For I am God alone.

3 Draw near to me my Zion,
For I am Judah's lion;
Oft times I hear you crying,
And listen to you mourn.
I never will forsake you—
I never will forget you,
No evil shall o'ertake you.
For I am God alone.

4 And if you lack for treasure,
Or if you lack for pleasure,
Or what is your desire,
Come quickly let it known.
I am the God of pleasure—
I am the God of treasure,
And there 's none that 's higher,
For I am God alone.

5 I am your friend and Father—
Your comforter and brother;
Love me and love no other—
My mercies all are known.
Forsake your worldly pleasures—
I will grant you treasures,
And grant your desire,
For I am God alone.

157.

L. M. REV. T. JONES

1 SINNERS! perhaps this news to you
May have no weight, although so true;
The carnal pleasures of the earth
Cast off the thoughts and fears of death.

2 The aged sinner will not turn!
His heart so hard he cannot mourn—
Much harder than the flinty rock—
He will not turn though Jesus knock.

3 The blooming youth, all in their prime,
Are counting out their length of time;
They often say 'tis their intent
When they get old they will repent.

4 But oh! the sad and awful state
Of those who stay and come too late!
The foolish virgins did begin
To knock, but could not enter in.

5 Then, parents, take a solemn view
Of your dear children—dear to you;
How can you bear to hear them cry,
And charge to you their misery?

6 When Christ, the Lord, shall come again,
In solemn pomp and burning flame—
Say, Gabriel! go proclaim the sound!
Awake ye nations under ground.

7 O, how will parents tremble there,
Who raised their children without prayer!
Methinks they'll hear their children say:
I never heard my parents pray!

8 Good Lord! what groans, what bitter cries!
What thunder rolling through the skies!
Poor sinners sink in dark despair,
While saints are shouting through the air.

158.

C. M.

Chief among Ten Thousand.

1 MAJESTIC sweetness sits enthron'd
Upon the Saviour's brow;
His head with radiant glories crowned,
His lips with grace o'erflow.

2 No mortal can with him compare,
Among the sons of men;
Fairer is he than all the fair,
Who fill the heavenly train.

3 He saw me plung'd in deep distress,
And flew to my relief;
For me he bore the shameful cross,
And carried all my grief.

4 Since from his bounty I receive
Such proofs of love divine;
Had I a thousand hearts to give—
Lord! they should all be thine.

159.

REV. T. JONES.

The Christian Soldier.

1 THE war in which the soldier fights
Is not the war for me;
By it are crushed all fond delights,
And sadness there I see.

But there 's a war—a holy strife,
By which is gained a blissful life
To all eternity.
O that 's the war for me,
O that 's the war for me.

2 The sword the crested warrior wields
Is not the sword for me;
While marching over tented fields
To death and victory.
But there 's a sword that pierces deep,
And often makes the sinner weep,
And to the Saviour flee.
O that 's the sword for me, &c.

3 The fame that 's gained by men of blood
Is not the fame for me;
By drenching earth in gory flood
Of friend and enemy.
But there 's a fame—a glory bright,
The christian soldier has in sight,
As onward marches he.
O that 's the fame for me, &c.

4 The wreath that twines the victor's brow
Is not the wreath for me;
For to receive it who would bow,
Save that through pride it be?

But there's a wreath—a shining crown,
To him who gains a blest renown,
To all eternity.
O that's the wreath for me, &c.

160.

Will you go?

1 WE'RE traveling home to heaven above,
Will you go, will you go?
To sing a Saviour's dying love,
Will you go, will you go?
Our sun will there no more go down,
Our moon no more will be withdrawn,
Our days of mourning past and gone—
Will you go, will you go?

2 We're going to walk the plains of light,
Will you go, will you go?
Where perfect day excludes the night,
Will you go, will you go?
The crown of life we there shall wear,
The palm of victory ever bear,
And all the joys of heaven share—
Will you go, will you go?

3 We're going to reap the rich reward,
Will you go, will you go?

Which Christ in heaven for us prepared,
Will you go, will you go?
A rich supply of milk and wine,
And everlasting joys divine,
And robes that will the sun outshine—
Will you go, will you go?

4 We 're going to strike the golden lyre,
Will you go, will you go?
And shout in strains of heavenly fire,
Will you go, will you go?
We 'll tell of God's redeeming grace,
And see our Saviour face to face,
And evermore will shout his praise—
Will you go, will you go?

5 The way to heaven is free for all,
Will you go, will you go?
Both Jew and Gentile, great and small,
Will you go, will you go?
Make up your minds—give God your heart,
From every sin and idol part,
And now for glory make a start—
Will you go, will you go?

6 The way to heaven is straight and plain,
Will you go, will you go?

Repent, believe, be born again,
Will you go, will you go?
The Saviour cries aloud to thee—
Take up thy cross and follow me,
You then shall my salvation see—
Will you go, will you go?

7 O could I hear some sinner say,
I will go, I will go;
I 'll start this moment—clear the way,
Let me go, let me go;
My old companions, fare you well,
I will not go with you to hell—
I mean with Jesus Christ to dwell—
Let me go—fare you well.

161.

JAMES A. CAVANAUGH.

The Turtle Dove.

1 HARK! do n't you hear the turtle dove,
The tokens of redeeming love?
From hill to hill we hear the sound,
The neighboring valleys echo round.
Oh Zion! hear the turtle dove—
The tokens of redeeming love;
They come the barren land to cheer,
And welcome in the jubile year.

2 The winter 's past—the rain is o'er—
We feel the chilling winds no more;
Sweet spring is come, and summer too—
All things appear divinely new.
On Zion's mount the watchmen cry:
The resurrection 's drawing nigh,
Behold the nations from abroad,
Are flocking to the mount of God.

162.

Death. L. M. J. Caitor.

1 I'M glad that I am born to die!
From grief and woe my soul shall fly;
Bright angels shall convey me home—
Away to New Jerusalem.

2 I'll praise him while he lends me breath—
I hope to praise him after death—
I hope to praise him when I die,
And shout salvation as I fly.

3 Farewell, vain world! I'm going home!
My Saviour smiles and bids me come;
Sweet angels beckon me away,
To sing God's praise in endless day.

4 I soon shall pass the vale of death,
And in his arms I'll lose my breath;

And then my happy soul shall tell—
My Jesus has done all things well.

5 I soon shall hear the awful sound:
Awake, ye nations, under ground!
Arise, and drop your dying shrouds!
And meet your Saviour in the clouds.

6 When to that blessed world I rise,
And join the anthems in the skies,
This note above the rest shall swell—
My Jesus has done all things well.

7 Then shall I see my blessed God,
And praise him in his bright abode;
My theme through all eternity,
Shall glory, glory, glory be.

163.

ASA NISWANGER.

1 COME listen to my story,
About the King of glory,
Whose garments were all gory,
And stained with blood.
Glory, hallelujah!

2 When I, by sin oppressed,
Was wretched and distressed,

Was guilty and depressed,
He saw my grief.
Glory, hallelujah!

3 But Satan had enrolled me,
And many a falsehood told me,
And said that he would hold me,
To serve him still.
Glory, hallelujah!

4 But I was not contented,
Though I had not repented,
And then my cries I vented—
Lord save my soul.
Glory, hallelujah!

5 And while I thus was crying,
I thought of crucifying,
And of my Saviour dying,
That I might live.
Glory, hallelujah!

6 I called on him to save me,
And oh, the look he gave me!
I thought that he did crave me,
To make me free.
Glory, hallelujah!

7 I heard him say, believe me,
And sin no more to grieve me,

And gladly now receive me,
And you shall be free.
Glory, hallelujah!

8 He cast his arms around me,
And broke the chains that bound me,
When he in bondage found me,
And I was free.
Glory, hallelujah!

9 So now I am loving Jesus,
Who in his mercy sees us,
And in distress frees us—
To him give praise.
Glory, hallelujah!

10 I 'll love him, hallelujah!
I 'll serve him, hallelujah!
I 'll praise him, hallelujah!
Praise ye the Lord.
Glory, hallelujah!

164. *Deliverance from Bondage.*

1 OUR bondage here shall end
Bye and bye—bye and bye;
Our griefs shall vanish then,
With our three-score years and ten,

And bright glory crown the day,
    Bye and bye—bye and bye.

2 When our Deliv'rer comes,
    Bye and bye—bye and bye;
From Egypt's yoke set free,
We will hail our jubilee,
And to Canaan all return,
    Bye and bye—bye and bye.

3 Though strong our foes appear,
    We 'll go on—we 'll go on;
Our hearts shall know no fear,
For Israel's God is near;
While the fiery pillar moves,
    We 'll go on—we 'll go on.

4 By Marah's bitter streams
    We 'll go on—we 'll go on;
Though Baca's vale be dry,
The rock shall yield supply;
To a land of corn and wine
    We 'll go on—we 'll go on.

5 And when to Jordan's flood
    We are come—we are come;
Jehovah rules the tide,
And the waters will divide,

While the ransom'd host shall shout,
We are come—we are come.

6 There friends shall meet again,
Who have loved—who have loved;
Our embraces shall be sweet,
When we each other greet
At our great Redeemer's feet,
Who have loved—who have loved.

7 There, with the happy throng,
We 'll rejoice—we 'll rejoice;
Shouting glory to our King,
Till the heavenly dome shall ring—
We 'll rejoice—we 'll rejoice.

165.

Free Grace.

1 THE voice of free grace
Cries, escape to the mountain;
For Adam's lost race
Christ hath open'd a fountain;
For sin and pollution,
And every transgression,
His blood flows most freely,
In streams of salvation.

CHORUS.

Hallelujah to the Lamb,
Who has purchased our pardon!
We will praise him again,
When we pass over Jordan.

2 Ye thirsty ones, hear it
With high exultation!
Behold! says the spirit,
The well of salvation;
Approach! cries the bride—
Lo! the multitudes going!
The soul-saving tide
To the nations is flowing.—*Chorus.*

3 Blest Jesus, ride on!
Thy kingdom is glorious;
O'er sin, death, and hell,
Thou wilt make us victorious.
Thy name shall be praised
In the great congregation,
And saints shall delight
In ascribing salvation.—*Chorus.*

4 When on Zion we stand,
Having gained the blest shore,
With our harps in our hands,
We will praise evermore;

We 'll range the blest fields
On the banks of the river,
And sing ballelujahs
Forever and ever.—*Chorus.*

166. *To the Sinful Youth.* P. M.

1 REMEMBER, sinful youth, you must die, you must die!
Remember, sinful youth, you must die;
Remember, sinful youth, who hate the ways of truth,
And in your pleasures boast, you must die, you must die,
And in your pleasures boast, you must die.

2 Uncertain are your days here below, here below,
Uncertain are your days, &c.;
Uncertain are your days, for God hath many ways
To bring you to your graves here below, here below,
To bring you to your graves, &c.

3 And if you travel down the broad road, the broad road,
And if you travel down, &c.;

And if you travel down, to darkness you are bound,
Eternally around the broad road, &c.,
Eternally around, &c.

4 To a dreadful judgment day you are bound, you are bound,
To a dreadful judgment day, &c.;
To a dreadful judgment day, be your tho'ts whate'er they may,
Nor can you it delay; you are bound, &c.,
Nor can you it delay, &c.

5 The God who built the sky, great I Am, great I Am,
The God who built the sky, &c.;
The God who built the sky hath said, and cannot lie:
Impenitence must die, and be damned, &c.,
Impenitence must die, &c.

6 And O, my friends, do n't you, I entreat, I entreat,
And O, my friends, &c.;
And O, my friends, do n't you your carnal mirth pursue,
Your guilty souls undo, I entreat, &c.,
Your guilty souls undo, &c.

7 Unto the Saviour flee—'scape for life,
'scape for life,
Unto the Saviour flee, &c.;
Unto the Saviour flee, lest death eternal be
Your final destiny—'scape for life, &c.,
Your final destiny, &c.

167. *The Cross.* L. M.

1 WHEN I survey the wond'rous cross
On which the Prince of glory died,
My richest gain I count but loss,
And pour contempt on all my pride.

2 Forbid it, Lord, that I should boast,
Save in the death of Christ, my God;
All the vain things that charm me most,
I sacrifice them to thy blood.

3 See, from his head, his hands, his feet,
Sorrow and love flow mingled down;
Did e'er such love and sorrow meet?
Or thorns compose so rich a crown?

4 Were the whole realm of nature mine,
That were a present far too small;
Love so amazing—so divine,
Demands my soul, my life, my all.

168.

MRS. LUCINDA PILCHER.

1 THOU art gone, little one, to a beautiful home,
Where no sickness can blight, where no sorrow can come;
Thy young spirit—too bright for this dark world of care,
Has been borne to a region all blissful and fair;
Thou was sent like a lovely and delicate flower,
To smile in our pathway one short, happy hour.

2 Then, as if this bleak world were too sterile and cold
For a blossom so fragile, its leaves to unfold,
The kind hand that nurtured thee bore thee away
To a sunnier clime in a region of day;
Already, we trust, thou hast joined a sweet band
Of the cherubim throng, in that bright spirit land.

3 They have swelled thy young spirit to
rapture ere this,
With their carol of joy, and their anthem
of bliss;
Now thy smile, in its gladness, no longer
shall bless
A fond mother, or answer thy father's
caress;
They have given thee back, in thy earliest
love,
To the Father in heaven—he claims thee
above.

4 They have yielded thee calmly—with
meekness and fear,
Though the message was sad, and the trial
severe;
Yet they gave thee, sweet child, to the arms
of thy God,
And submissively bowed to his chastening
rod.
Happy child! thou 'lt not need a fond
mother again,
To calm thee in sorrow, or soothe thee in
pain,

Since the Saviour so sweetly hath laid thee
to rest,
And pillowed thy head on his own faithful
breast.

169.

C. M. W. Alfred.

The happy Sick Man.

1 SWEET rivers of redeeming love
Lie just before mine eye;
Had I the pinions of a dove,
I'd to those rivers fly.
I'd rise superior to my pain—
With joy outstrip the wind;
I'd cross bold Jordan's stormy main,
And leave the world behind.

2 While I'm imprisoned here below,
In anguish, pain and smart,
Oft-times those troubles I forego,
When love surrounds my heart.
In darkest shadows of the night,
Faith mounts the upper sky;
I then behold my heart's delight,
And would rejoice to die.

3 I view the monster death and smile—
Now he has lost his sting;

Though Satan rages all the while,
I still in triumph sing.
I hold my Saviour in my arms,
And will not let him go;
I'm so delighted with his charms,
No other good I'll know.

4 A few more days or years, at most,
My troubles will be o'er;
I hope to join the heavenly host
On Canaan's happy shore.
My rapturous soul shall drink and feast
In love's unbounded sea—
The glorious hope of endless rest
Is now transporting me.

5 O come, my Saviour, come away,
And bear me through the sky!
Nor let thy chariot wheels delay—
Make haste and bring it nigh.
I long to see thy glorious face,
And in thine image shine—
To triumph in victorious grace,
And be forever thine.

www.ingramcontent.com/pod-product-compliance
Lightning Source LLC
LaVergne TN
LVHW050524100826
845148LV00002B/436

* 9 7 8 1 4 2 5 5 2 0 0 5 2 *